# A PRACTICAL GUIDE TO SCIENTIFIC AND TECHNICAL TRANSLATION
Publishing, Style and Terminology

**Other Books by James Brian Alexander Mitchell:**

*Dissociative Recombination: Theory, Experiment and Applications*
*Dissociative Recombination: Theory, Experiment and Applications II*
*Dissociative Recombination: Theory, Experiment and Applications III*
*Dissociative Recombination: Theory, Experiment and Applications IV*
*Atomic Collisions: Heavy Particle Projectiles*
*Abstracts of Papers: 19th International Conference on Electronic and Atomic Collisions (ICPEAC)*
*Electronic and Atomic Collisions: Invited Papers of the 19th ICPEAC*


**Books Translated by Anca Irina Florescu-Mitchell:**

**English to Romanian**

*Albert Einstein and the Frontiers of Physics*
*Why People Believe Weird Things*
*The Three Trillion Dollar War*
*The Unfinished Game*
*Is God a Mathematician?*
*Quantum Man – Richard Feynman's Life in Science*
*The Emperor's New Mind*

**English to French**

*Nightsky*
*Iceberg*
*A Day at the Gallery*
*Who am I?*

# A PRACTICAL GUIDE TO SCIENTIFIC AND TECHNICAL TRANSLATION
Publishing, Style and Terminology

**James Brian Alexander Mitchell**
*University of Rennes I, France (Retired Professor)*
*MERL-Consulting SAS, France*

**Anca Irina Florescu-Mitchell**
*MERL-Consulting SAS, France*

*Published by*

World Scientific Publishing Co. Pte. Ltd.
5 Toh Tuck Link, Singapore 596224
*USA office:* 27 Warren Street, Suite 401-402, Hackensack, NJ 07601
*UK office:* 57 Shelton Street, Covent Garden, London WC2H 9HE

**Library of Congress Cataloging-in-Publication Data**
Names: Mitchell, J. B. A. (J. Brian A.), author. | Florescu-Mitchell, Anca Irina, author.
Title: A practical guide to scientific and technical translation : publishing, style and terminology / James Brian Alexander Mitchell, Anca Irina Florescu-Mitchell.
Description: New Jersey : World Scientific, [2022] | Includes bibliographical references and index.
Identifiers: LCCN 2021049420 | ISBN 9789811241550 (hardcover) |
  ISBN 9789811243141 (paperback) | ISBN 9789811241567 (ebook for institutions) |
  ISBN 9789811241574 (ebook for individuals)
Subjects: LCSH: Science--Translating--Handbooks, manuals, etc. | Technology--Translating--Handbooks, manuals, etc. | Technical writing--Handbooks, manuals, etc.
Classification: LCC Q124 .M58 2022 | DDC 501/.4--dc23/eng/20211216
LC record available at https://lccn.loc.gov/2021049420

**British Library Cataloguing-in-Publication Data**
A catalogue record for this book is available from the British Library.

Copyright © 2022 by World Scientific Publishing Co. Pte. Ltd.

*All rights reserved. This book, or parts thereof, may not be reproduced in any form or by any means, electronic or mechanical, including photocopying, recording or any information storage and retrieval system now known or to be invented, without written permission from the publisher.*

For photocopying of material in this volume, please pay a copying fee through the Copyright Clearance Center, Inc., 222 Rosewood Drive, Danvers, MA 01923, USA. In this case permission to photocopy is not required from the publisher.

For any available supplementary material, please visit
https://www.worldscientific.com/worldscibooks/10.1142/12404#t=suppl

Desk Editor: Shaun Tan Yi Jie

Typeset by Stallion Press
Email: enquiries@stallionpress.com

Printed in Singapore

# Authors' Note

This book has been written jointly by James Brian Alexander Mitchell (JBAM) and Anca Irina Florescu-Mitchell (AIFM) and so when we refer to a particular subject we use the word "we". For example, "We have seen that French authors…", "We usually translate the word as…", and so on. When there is a section that deals specifically with our individual experiences, we indicate who is "speaking" by adding (JBAM) or (AIFM).

JBAM has always written articles in English and regularly translates from French to English. AIFM has written articles in English and wrote her thesis in French. She translates French to English, English to French, and English/French to Romanian (and occasionally vice versa).

Hence this book uses French as its language of discussion. Examples are given in French and English. For this we apologise to those readers who are not perhaps familiar with French but who may find similar ideas when translating from their own language. To try to give examples in German, Spanish, Dutch, Swedish, Chinese, Swahili or Japanese would just be pretending that we know these languages (JBAM knows a few words of Swahili) and we would probably be committing awful errors.

The first part of the book is dedicated to Direct Authoring. To the scientist who has to write an article in English (though some examples are in French), the main goal is how to avoid pitfalls (grammar errors or incorrect meanings) when writing their paper.

The second part is directed more to the technical translator who is faced with a text on a particular subject and may need some guidance on how to find the right terminology. Again, our experience is in the French-English pair. Hence the target language (the language you are translating into) is predominantly English. This means that a translator from another "source" language should be able to get some help from this section, if they are translating into English.

Finally, a word about format. When we use a word or phrase in *French*, we shall write it in italics. When we use a word or phrase in English, we shall use normal script. In addition, we have adopted a conversational tone in this book to make it more readable but in general, when writing or translating technical documents, a more formal tone is required and this is one of the areas that we shall discuss, particularly in the first part of the book, devoted to Direct Authoring.

# About the Authors

**Dr. James Brian Alexander Mitchell** retired as Professeur (Class Exceptionelle) at the Université de Rennes I, France in 2017. He was previously Professor at the University of Western Ontario, Canada from 1980–1996, where he served concurrently as Director of the Centre for Interdisciplinary Studies in Chemical Physics and Chairman of Graduate Affairs in the Department of Physics. Since 2018, he is CEO of Merl-Consulting, a firm that provides consulting and translation services. He holds a PhD and BSc Hons. (1st Class) in Physics from Queen's University Belfast, Northern Ireland.

As Professor of Physics for almost 40 years in Canada and France, Dr. Mitchell published over 120 scientific papers and co-authored/edited 7 books. He has also provided over 70 reviews for *Physical Review, Physical Review Letters* as well as many other scientific journals, and given over 80 invited talks at conferences and universities in North America, Europe and the Middle East. His research areas were in X-ray scattering, atomic/molecular collisions, dissociative recombination, and combustion. He won the Innocentive Solver-of-the-Year Award, USA in 2007 and holds 3 patents in the automotive and oil industries.

Since retiring, Dr. Mitchell has specialised in French-to-English technical translations of patent reports, patents, technical manuals, technical specifications, scientific theses and journal articles for automobile and aircraft manufacturing companies and the oil industry in North America and France. His clients have included Airbus Industries (formerly EADS), Peugeot, EDF, Total, US Air Force, Imperial Oil Resources Ltd., and EXXON Chemical Co. amongst others. He currently offers the following training courses — *Technical translation: Finding the right terminology* and *Tips for technical translations*.

**Dr. Anca Irina Florescu-Mitchell** is a specialist trilingual translator since 2005, with experience in scientific translation and consulting in Romanian, French and English. She obtained her PhD from the University of Paris XI, with her thesis written in French. During her 12 years of experience as a researcher in Physics at University of Pittsburgh, USA, Institute for Space Sciences, Romania, University Paris VI and University Rennes 1, France, she naturally achieved the ability of writing scientific papers directly in French and English, and her knowledge of the scientific and technical vocabulary in both languages is wide and profound. She is currently President of Merl-Consulting, a firm that provides consulting and translation services.

Dr. Florescu-Mitchell's translation expertise is extensive. She has translated 7 English books into Romanian, including *Albert Einstein and the Frontiers of Physics, Quantum Man — Richard Feynman's Life in Science*, and *The Emperor's New Mind*. From Romanian to English, she has translated press releases, geotechnical reports, construction manuals and railway transportation texts. Her English-to-French and French-to-English translation works include patents, patent reports, technical manuals, press releases, newsletters, websites and contracts in a variety of disciplines such as environmental, nuclear, mechanical engineering, automobile, defense, medical, pharmaceutical, cosmetic, oil and gas, mining, construction, inter alia. Finally, she provides translation of technical manuals and contracts from French to Romanian for the machine tool and automotive industries.

# Contents

*Authors' Note* v
*About the Authors* vii

## Chapter 1 Scientific Translation for Authors 1

1.1 Introduction 1
    1.1.1 First, a personal note (JBAM) 4
    1.1.2 Generalities 5
1.2 Direct Authoring 7
    1.2.1 Which English to use (UK or US) 8
    1.2.2 Do's and Don'ts 10
    1.2.3 Passive versus active voice 12
    1.2.4 Present tense, past tense, future tense 13
    1.2.5 Plurals 15
    1.2.6 "-ing" forms: nouns (gerunds) and verbs (present participles) 17
    1.2.7 Adjectives 19
    1.2.8 Adverbs 20
    1.2.9 Prepositions 21
    1.2.10 Words used incorrectly 23
    1.2.11 Allow, enable, permit 29
    1.2.12 "The" and "a" 30
    1.2.13 "In" and "into", "on" and "onto" 33
    1.2.14 "This" and "that" 34

|       1.2.15 "Of" and "off"                                     | 35 |
|       1.2.16 Gender-neutral text                                | 37 |
|       1.2.17 Numbers                                            | 40 |
|       1.2.18 Punctuation                                        | 40 |
|       1.2.19 Phrasing (word order)                              | 43 |
|       1.2.20 Sentence style                                     | 45 |
|       1.2.21 Machine translation                                | 46 |
|   1.3 Final Word                                                | 48 |
|   1.4 Feedback (rex) from non-French-speaking Colleagues        | 49 |

## Chapter 2  Reviewing — 52

|   2.1 Introduction     | 52 |
|   2.2 Misunderstandings| 53 |

## Chapter 3  Technical Translation for Translators — 56

|   3.1 Introduction                                              | 56 |
|   3.2 Tools of the Trade                                        | 60 |
|       3.2.1 Spelling and grammar checkers                       | 62 |
|   3.3 Computer Aided Translation (CAT) Tools                    | 63 |
|       3.3.1 Q&A                                                 | 64 |
|       3.3.2 Translation memories and consistency                | 65 |
|       3.3.3 Termbases and consistency                           | 66 |
|       3.3.4 Agencies, translation memories, termbases and packages | 68 |
|       3.3.5 Technical problems with CAT tools                   | 69 |
|   3.4 Machine Translation                                       | 71 |
|   3.5 Internet Searching                                        | 75 |

## Chapter 4  Specific Technical Fields — 79

|   4.1 Abbreviations/Acronyms                                    | 79 |
|       4.1.1 Use of acronyms in scientific publications          | 80 |
|   4.2 Physics                                                   | 83 |
|       4.2.1 Fundamental differences                             | 84 |
|       4.2.2 Exercises                                           | 88 |

|  |  |
|---|---|
| 4.3 Chemistry | 88 |
|     4.3.1 Exercises | 91 |
| 4.4 Aeronautics | 92 |
|     4.4.1 Exercises | 97 |
| 4.5 Automotive Engineering | 97 |
|     4.5.1 Exercises | 101 |
| 4.6 Railways and Trams | 102 |
|     4.6.1 Exercises | 109 |
| 4.7 Mechanical Engineering | 109 |
|     4.7.1 Mechanical structures | 111 |
|     4.7.2 Welding and soldering | 112 |
|     4.7.3 Bolted (screwed) assemblies | 114 |
|     4.7.4 Standards | 116 |
|     4.7.5 Testing | 118 |
|     4.7.6 Special terminology | 118 |
|     4.7.7 Exercises | 121 |
| 4.8 Construction | 122 |
|     4.8.1 Exercises | 125 |
| 4.9 Nuclear Engineering | 125 |
|     4.9.1 Exercises | 130 |
| 4.10 Renewable Energy | 130 |
|     4.10.1 Exercises | 135 |
| 4.11 Hydroelectric Power and Hydraulic Engineering | 135 |
|     4.11.1 Exercises | 140 |
| 4.12 Insurance | 141 |
| 4.13 Patents | 144 |
|     4.13.1 Exercises | 147 |
| 4.14 Contracts and Legal/Financial Translation | 147 |
|     4.14.1 Exercises | 150 |

## Chapter 5 Translation As A Profession    151

| | |
|---|---|
| 5.1 General Issues Facing the Translator: Problems Encountered | 151 |
|     5.1.1 The client thinks your translation is too literal | 152 |
|     5.1.2 We wanted something sexy... | 153 |

|  |  |
|---|---|
| 5.1.3 That is not how we say it | 153 |
| 5.1.4 You made a mistake in the title | 153 |
| 5.1.5 You made a spelling error on page 93 | 154 |
| 5.1.6 You did not correct the Franglais in the source text (even though you were not paid to do so, and not even asked) | 154 |
| 5.1.7 You told us you could do legal translations, but you don't use standard legal terminology | 155 |
| 5.1.8 You used UK English but we wanted US English. Didn't we tell you. I am sure we did… | 155 |
| 5.1.9 I don't think this was translated by a native English speaker | 156 |
| 5.1.10 I think the translator used machine translation | 157 |
| 5.1.11 The client pays the agency, but the agency does not pay you | 159 |
| 5.1.12 You did the translation but the client does not exist | 160 |
| 5.1.13 The client overpays you and asks for you to return some of the money | 161 |
| 5.2 Where to Find Work? | 162 |
| *Final Words* | 163 |
| *Additional Reading* | 165 |
| *Answers to Exercises* | 166 |
| *Appendix I* | 169 |
| *Appendix II* | 170 |

# Chapter 1

# Scientific Translation for Authors

## 1.1 Introduction

*"This is not a love song. I don't sing my mother tongue."*

— Rammstein's "Amerika"

Writing an article in a language that is not your own is difficult. You are used to planning what you are going to say, introducing the topic, presenting your data and framing your arguments, in your own language. Now you have to write all this in English. So you have to transpose all this in your mind as you put pen to paper. You have to start thinking about vocabulary, grammar, how an English speaker would say this. (This is a level of difficulty that is often the reason that non-English-speaking scientists procrastinate when it comes to getting to work on their papers). And after you have done all this and sent in the paper to the journal, the referee report that comes back includes the dreaded phrase: "The English in this paper needs serious rework!"

One of the motivations in writing this book is to try to help you avoid some of the pitfalls of scientific writing in English so that you may sail through this obstacle to getting your fine work published. You might still have to ask a tame English speaker to help you but at least the major work will have been done.

First of all, we must say that this is not a textbook. In fact, the inspiration for this book comes from REX (a word used extensively in

French technical and business literature). REX is short for *Retour d'expérience*, often translated as "feedback" but a better translation is "operating experience" — the experience you have picked up by working in the field. Hence when writing this book, we have used examples of what we have encountered, whether in helping colleagues to improve their manuscripts or when doing translations of technical documents in a wide variety of fields.

The book is intended for people who care about how they express their ideas and who understand that good science is language sensitive. Science is about knowledge but also about communication, ideally without the distortion introduced by over-simplification (which is what popular science magazines do) or jargon (often used by authors who have nothing to say). It has been said that the best theory book is without formulae. We doubt it. The truth is that, if something can be conveyed by beautiful mathematics, it will be and people would be just as happy to read formulae. However, science is not mathematics. It deals with ideas, some old, some new, some right, some wrong, which have to be discussed and interpreted.

We assume that you, as readers, have done your homework when you were kids and that you loved grammar. So this is not intended to be a grammar book. It deals with equivalences from one language to another, emphasising the importance of avoiding common errors, something machine translation is not yet, and may never be, able to do.

English is the most spoken foreign language in the world, one of the reasons being that its grammar is rather simple, and it is relatively easy to make yourself understood when you speak. Native English speakers are used to speaking with many different nationalities with differing accents, so generally they have less difficulties in understanding a non-native English speaker, than perhaps is the case with other language pairs. However, written English is considered to be difficult and when it is scientific English, there are many, not necessarily obvious, rules that one must follow. Emphasis will be placed in this book on explaining these rules and on helping you to avoid the common mistakes that are invariably seen.

The authors of this book spend much of their working lives these days doing technical translations, usually of an engineering nature.

Thus, we shall also develop this topic with examples from different sectors, especially those that have very specific vocabularies. For example, in aviation, English is the common language of pilots internationally and one of the secrets of success in this endeavour is that the terms that are used by pilots and air traffic controllers are always standard. When you do an aviation translation, you better have your aviation dictionary open beside you because guessing the translation can have serious consequences for safety. In addition, patent writing is very specific with many rules for presenting the invention in the most neutral and specific fashion. We shall deal with this as well as with other sectors that we regularly translate in.

One cannot and should not do everything and so there are sectors that we shall not cover, from a straight translation viewpoint, these being beyond our knowledge skills. We shall not discuss biological and medical translations, which are areas that have their own language, nomenclature and terminologies. This book is aimed at Physics, Chemistry and Engineering practitioners primarily, though general rules for scientific publishing may be of assistance to scientists in other fields.

The authors usually work in the French-English language pair but we have asked colleagues who are native speakers of other languages to comment on our material and to highlight specific difficulties that they may have when they set out to write in English. We shall include this feedback in the book and shall discuss problems that we have seen in work produced by different language speakers.

One of us (JBAM) was very frustrated when first moving to France by being constantly corrected every time that he opened his mouth to speak. Eventually he had to ask that this had to stop because of the embarrassment that it caused him. Humility is a very necessary virtue when you are talking about language and we hope that the spirit of this book will be one of positive assistance. You should never feel embarrassed if you ask a colleague to read over your work, nor be frustrated if it comes back with lots of red ink. They probably are not able to write very well (if at all) in your language.

So, in summary, we hope that you find this book useful and would be very interested to get your feedback (through the publisher) so that we may be able to answer specific questions you may have that have gone unanswered.

## 1.1.1 *First, a personal note (JBAM)*

My introduction to translation was when I arrived in Canada as a postdoctoral research fellow at the University of Western Ontario. I was joining a group that had developed a new apparatus for measuring the recombination of electrons and molecular ions and the group had obtained its first results a couple of months before my arrival. The Head of the group had written a first draft of a paper on this subject and my job was to turn this paper into readable English. Thus, my very first publication was in *Physical Review Letters* but I am not listed as one of the authors, just as an acknowledgement. However, that gave me a real taste for writing and presenting scientific results.

After 20 years in North America, I moved to France and became a Professor at the Université de Rennes I in the beautiful region of Brittany. Over the next 20 years I was often called upon by my colleagues to help them sort out problems in their papers that they encountered when a referee asked for an improvement in the English. After retiring from the University, I decided to continue this theme by doing technical translations, again with the occasional work of correcting the English in scientific papers. My wife Anca (AIFM), the co-author of this book, had been doing technical translations for a number of years and so this became a partnership in the adventure. Like many of her countrymen and women, she had learned French from a very young age. Romania is a country that uses a Latin-based language. There has been a long history of French speaking in that country even though the language itself has more affinity with both Italian and Catalan. Anca translates from English to French and vice versa but also into Romanian (she has translated a number of popular science books in Romanian).

Ultimately, the secret of producing a good document, whether in English or in another language, is to have a wide knowledge of your field and to read as much as you can in the target language — the language that you are translating into. I was surprised when my children displayed a good knowledge of English even though I had always spoken French to them. I was particularly insistent that they speak French properly as it is a language where few mistakes are accepted. In fact, they had picked up English by watching DVD videos with us with English or French subtitles. Thus, they had become accustomed to hearing and understanding English without the usual feeling of it being a chore imposed by their school. I really recommend this simple and enjoyable technique and with modern technology, you are offered a very wide range of subtitling languages to help you with this effort.

### 1.1.2 *Generalities*

Back in the 1970's, when JBAM was starting out on his research career, you could go to an international scientific conference and listen to talks given in English, French, German, Russian, and Spanish. Nowadays, these conferences are almost exclusively held in English. Even national conferences and meetings are often held in English at least in part. English has become the lingua franca of science and technology and so the primary emphasis in this work will be to help you to produce the best possible document in English. Nevertheless, we shall try not to ignore the possibility of writing in and translating into other languages and shall talk a little about the various nuances that can be found when doing this.

This book is not intended as a test of English grammar and vocabulary. The reader is considered to have a basic knowledge of English, at least to be able to read this book! What we are setting out to do is to provide a guide to scientific style, how to avoid the standard problems that arise when you write in English. The ultimate goal for some readers will be to get their papers accepted by referees and editors without the often-cited phrase: "The English in this document needs substantial revision."

As a foreign language, or as we prefer to say, a "source" language, our experience is mainly French (Romanian and French for AIFM). In fact, many of the errors in transposition from French into the "target" English language are common to European languages and so this specific case in itself is not a real handicap for the non-French-speaking European reader.

This book is not just addressed to scientific authors publishing in English-language journals. It is also targeted at translators, faced with technical and scientific documents. Thus, we have included sections regarding various engineering sectors and a small section will be devoted to patent translation, which is a very important area with its own very specific rules.

We shall also speak of the topic dreaded by many translators, namely machine translation (MT). It is very tempting for people who are direct authoring in English to call upon Google Translate or other translation tools to produce their documents. This can have appalling consequences in scientific publications if it is not done by an MT professional and post-edited by a skilled translator. But more about that later. For now, let us begin with Do's and Don'ts when preparing a scientific paper for publication.

> "The difficulties of language are not negligible. One's native speech is a closely fitting garment, and one never feels quite at ease when it is not immediately available and has to be replaced by another. My thanks are due to Dr Inkster (Trinity College, Dublin), to Dr Padraig Browne (St Patrick's College, Maynooth) and, last but not least, to Mr S. C. Roberts. They were put to great trouble to fit the new garment on me and to even greater trouble by my occasional reluctance to give up some "original" fashion of my own. Should some of it have survived the mitigating tendency of my friend, it is to be put at my door, not at theirs."
>
> — Erwin Schrödinger, Dublin 1944

> "To put this collection together, I came up against a problem to which I must draw the reader's attention. Some of my articles were written directly in English and so they had to be translated [Translator's note: into French]. However, during the course of this work, I was struck by the difference in tone and composition between the texts conceived in one or other of the languages. The result is a heterogeneity that I fear, compromises the equilibrium and unity of the work.

*(Continued)*

> The origin of this difference can be partly explained sociologically: you do not think or express yourself in the same way when you address a French speaking or an English-speaking audience. There are also personal reasons, however. Irrespective of my familiarity with the English language, in which I have taught for several years, I use it incorrectly and with a limited range. I think in English what I write in this language, yet without always realising it, I say what I can, and not what I want, with the linguistic means at my disposal. Hence the sentiment of strangeness that I feel in the presence of my own texts, when I try to re-transcribe them into French."
>
> — *Translated from: Claude Levy-Strauss,* Anthroplogie structurale, *Préface, Pocket, Plon, 2016 (The original in French is given in Appendix I)*

## 1.2 Direct Authoring

When you sit down to write an article for publication, you are essentially faced with a number of choices. Direct authoring in English, drafting in your own language followed by translation either by yourself or someone else, and more recently using machine translation. We shall deal with these three choices individually, but we shall start with direct authoring. This is where you write directly in English having collected your thoughts and having decided on the structure and content of your article. This is probably the most popular way to approach the problem, at least for European authors.

But how will you structure your article? What approach should you take to make it attractive, interesting, and relevant to the reader? Why are you writing it? Okay, you need publications so you can get that promotion but at least try to make them readable. Before starting, you should ask yourself several questions:

- What is my story?
- What message do I want to get across?
- Do I understand what we have done?

(Sorry, this book cannot help you with the third question.)

(JBAM) As a native English speaker, answering the first two questions is a relatively easy task and I can concentrate on the scientific content and how to tell my story in as compact and interesting a way as possible. For the non-native English speaker, there is now the challenge of how to express yourself as clearly as possible with what may or may not be a limited knowledge of the subtleties of English scientific publication. Having been called upon by many of my (French) colleagues to improve the English in their submitted papers, I often suggested to them to write the article first in their own language and then I could translate it for them. In this way I would be able to understand what exactly they wanted to say. I also made a suggestion to the editorial board of a well-known physics journal that they should publish two versions of articles from non-English speaking authors, one in English and the other in their native language. In this way, one would be sure to have the exact meaning of their text. I don't think this suggestion was ever implemented.

Let's move on to the technical issues involved in publishing scientific material in English. By saying technical, we are speaking about the "Do's and Don'ts" as well as about style, grammar and convention. As mentioned earlier, this book is not a course in grammar or vocabulary but all the same, we shall touch upon these where appropriate. One of the most useful resources for scientific writing can be found in the American Physical Society's "Reviews of Modern Physics Style Guide" with an appendix "WRITING A BETTER SCIENTIFIC ARTICLE" by Karie Friedman, Assistant Editor, *Reviews of Modern Physics*. This contains much useful information particularly with regard to errors in grammar and English usage in general. In this chapter we shall highlight some of the content of this document along with other observations gained from personal experiences and basic rules learned.

### 1.2.1 *Which English to use (UK or US)*

Like many languages, there are many different versions of English but for the purposes of publication we shall stick to just two: UK English and US English.

Obviously, you should choose your version according to the nationality of the journal you wish to publish in. In fact, generally anyone used to reading in one version will have little difficulty with the other but publishers are picky so you should adjust your text accordingly.

The main differences are "s" vs "z":

> "organisation" (UK) vs "organization" (US)
> "analyse" (UK) vs "analyze" (US),

and "ou" (UK) vs "o" (US):

> "behaviour" (UK) vs "behavior" (US).

The best thing is to set your spellchecker to the appropriate language before starting. However, some things are not so obvious:

> "defence" (UK) vs "defense" (US)
> "aeroplane" (UK) vs "airplane" (US)
> "grey" (UK) vs "gray" (US)
> "lorry" (UK) vs "truck" (US)
> "aluminium" (UK) vs "aluminum" (US).

Fortunately, there are lots of websites that list the most common distinctions so check out UK English vs US English and see which one suits you the best.

The most complicated issue concerns units. If you are writing a scientific article, it is best to stay with the *Système International (SI)* units, namely:

> "metre" (UK) or "meter" (US)
> "kilogram" or "kilogramme" (UK) or "kilogram" (US),

etc. On the other hand, for an engineering article in US English, you might need to change to miles, feet, inches, and pounds (lb). Again, you can find lots of websites offering conversions from one to the other.

There is, nevertheless, one little point you may or may not be familiar with: the difference between kilograms and pounds. Oh, that is easy, you will say, as my conversion website tells me that:

$$1 \text{ kilogram (kg)} = 2.20462 \text{ pounds (lb)}.$$

In reality, it is not so simple for the kilogram is a unit of mass while the pound is a unit of force. By convention we talk about weight in kilograms but you should actually talk about weight in Newtons where:

$$1 \text{ kg} = 9.81 \text{ N}.$$

The UK unit of mass is the "slug", where 1 slug = 32.2 lb, the acceleration of gravity being 32.2 ft/s$^2$. This is rarely seen in the literature.

Just something to keep in mind.

### 1.2.2 Do's and Don'ts

The title of this paragraph is rather amusing, for in a scientific article you don't use:

"don't", "it's", "they'll"

or any contraction. You should write:

"do not", "it is", they will",

etc. But you will say, "my English teacher taught us to speak like this!" Indeed, she or he may have done this but the operative word in this sentence is "speak". You can use these in spoken English but should not in written English. Oh, and another thing, you shouldn't start a written sentence with "But". This is too direct for written work. You could use "However," at the start of a sentence but even here, it is better to embed it in the text. For example:

"The fact is, however, that high intensity x-rays can cause serious damage to materials."

Putting "However," at the start of the sentence turns it into a conversation rather than a statement of facts.

There are other words that should not be used in scientific writing:

"enough".

The use of this word is badly seen. One should rephrase the sentence to use the word:

"sufficient".

For example:

"For $\mu$ large enough"

should be rephrased as:

"For sufficiently large $\mu$".

Why is this so? Well, the word "enough" is scientifically vague. How much is enough? (How much money is ever enough?) The word "sufficient", on the other hand, is clear; it means the smallest amount required. You do not need more, it is "sufficient".

You should also avoid using "like", for example:

"Like Smith and Smith explained in their article".

Rather, say:

"As Smith and Smith explained in their article".

This type of phrasing using "enough" and "like" is considered as being very colloquial and again rather conversational.

Similarly, avoid the word "big":

"The apparatus used is very big."

Rather, use:

"The apparatus used is very large."

Again, there is a subtlety here. You would say:

> "It would cost a large amount of money",

not

> "It would cost a big amount of money".

"Big" has a colloquial ring to it and colloquial expressions are to be avoided when writing. Moreover, "large" expresses the size but not the weight of the apparatus. To say an apparatus is "big" gives the impression that it could fall and crush you. It should be noted that in French "large" means "wide", so here we have somewhat of a *faux-ami* (false friend, i.e., incorrect translation of a similar sounding word or incorrectly chosen synonym). So be careful.

Having said all this, there are always exceptions and one that has come into common usage is "big data"!

### 1.2.3 *Passive versus active voice*

Here is a question that you always have to ask yourself when writing your article. When do you include yourself (I) or your colleagues (we) in the text? Generally speaking, scientific articles should be written in the passive voice:

> "The experiment was performed"

rather than the active voice:

> "We performed the experiment"

and you would very rarely say:

> "I performed the experiment".

Referring to yourself makes the article too personal and maybe you have gotten things wrong! Using the passive voice protects you from such criticism and using the active "we" (even if it is the "royal we")[1] implies a spirit of collaboration. All the same, this is not a hard and fast rule and sometimes it is quite appropriate to use "we". A specific example of this will be given in the next segment as a good way of avoiding one of the most basic errors that a non-native speaker can make.

Adopting the active voice can make a paper more readable and, in some circumstances, it may be essential to identify who did what.

(JBAM) I once rejected a Master's Degree thesis because I could not understand what the student had done and if he had in fact done anything? He had written it in a completely passive voice, and it read like a description of work done by others. He re-wrote the thesis and it was then clear that he was a brilliant student who had well merited his diploma. I felt bad about this, but I had been called upon as an external examiner to grade the merits of the document and to me I could not understand what its author had achieved.

### 1.2.4 *Present tense, past tense, future tense*

When you write in English, and you are describing an experiment that you have performed or a calculation you have made, you always use the past tense.

> "The ion beam and electron beam were merged, and measurements of the dissociative recombination were performed."

> "Potential energy curves were calculated using the XXX software."

Often in French writings, you find that the authors use the present tense when describing such events.

> *Les faisceaux sont mis en confluence et les mesures de recombinaison dissociative sont réalisées.*

---

[1] Kings and Queens use the word "we" when they speak, for they are in fact speaking on behalf of their people. This is called the "royal we".

> (The beams are brought into confluence and the dissociative recombination measurements are carried out.)

This is very perturbing for an English reader. Have they done it? Are they going to do it? What?

Similarly, if you are writing a proposal for doing an experiment or carrying out a research project, you must use the future tense:

> "The apparatus will be built and tested"

or the present indefinite tense:

> "We propose carrying out calculations".

Do not use the present tense to describe the apparatus, such as:

> "The apparatus has an electron gun and ion optics for forming the beam".

Instead you should write:

> "The apparatus will have an electron gun and ion optics for forming the beam".

Sometimes there is an imperative that must be addressed. Do not say:

> "All safety precautions are taken to ensure that no one is present in the instrument hutch".[2]

Instead:

> "All safety precautions shall be taken to ensure that no one is present in the instrument hutch".

Here "shall" is used to indicate the imperative nature of the sentence.

---

[2] For the reader not familiar with synchrotron radiation facilities, check out the word "hutch" on the Internet. (Clue: it does not refer to a rabbit's house!)

> "All safety precautions will be taken to ensure that
> no one is present in the instrument hutch".

This is more a way of assuring the reader that the precautions will be taken. If there is a strict imperative, then one would say:

> "Everyone must leave the experimental hutch
> before the x-ray beam shutter is opened".

## 1.2.5 *Plurals*

This is something that often shows up in articles written by a non-native English speaker. In fact, there are two problems: not using plurals when you should and using them when you should not. In French for example, the "s" at the end of a plural noun is generally not pronounced. It is often found in articles where the French author has thought about what they want to say but when they write it, they forget about the "s" in English because they do not hear it. At least that is what seems to happen. If they have an adjective or a definite article associated with the noun, in French they would be sure to use the correct plural form such as:

> *Les électrons rapides produits par le filament*

but when they convert into English, it might come out as:

> "The fast electron produced by the filament"

because they have not heard the "s" in their heads. Just remember, if it is plural, do not forget the "s". Just like in French!

However, some words in English are always singular. Common examples are:

> "information"
> "equipment"

so

> "information is always transmitted"

and never:

"informations are transmitted".

Similarly,

"the equipment is in place"

and never:

"the equipments are in place".

To express these items in singular form, you could say "piece (or item) of equipment" and "piece (or item) of information".

But not all plurals end with "s"! These are mainly irregular forms that are learned by heart in school (children, men, women, teeth, etc.) and we will not talk about them here. We will just give you a small exercise at the end of this section.

To pile on the confusion, there are words which are treated as plural in English and singular in French. For example:

"personnel"

is plural in English. Thus:

"The personnel are trained in their respective jobs".

But in French, the word *personnel* is treated like a block. Thus, a singular word. An interesting example of this dichotomy between French and English can be found in a sentence such as the following:

"A majority of blocks do not contain an outlier"
(Taken from an article on statistics).

Note that the verb "do" is plural as we refer to the blocks, a plural noun, and not to the "majority". The French would be:

*La majorité des blocs ne contient pas des valeurs aberrantes.*

The verb *contient* has the singular conjugation as it refers to the "majority", a singular noun. Another example:

"A bunch of electrons pass through the target"

and not

> "A bunch of electrons passes through the target".

Whoever told you English was easy?

Exercise: Just to get used to checking plural forms, find the plural form for:

> plateau
> fish
> life
> formula
> radius
> quantum

(NB: if you know your Latin, the last three ones should not be a problem!)

> phenomenon
> basis
> criterion

(NB: and if you know your Greek, no problem for these last three!)

## 1.2.6 "-ing" forms: nouns (gerunds) and verbs (present participles)

A more unusual plural (and hardly mentioned anywhere as it is more a problem of understanding than of direct grammar) is the use of a gerund to name a set. For example, if a system is being tested, you can say:

> "the system was undergoing several tests"

or:

> "the system was undergoing testing".

Here, "testing" is the gerund, and has the meaning of "a set of tests". As an empirical rule, a gerund as a plural names an action which is a set of several "normal" nouns ("searching" can be a set of "searches", "publishing" a set of "publications", etc.). In such cases, you can be sure that "searchings" and "publishings" are incorrect. Yet when there is no noun perfectly equivalent to a gerund, as in "finding", the plural exists ("Our findings will be soon published"). A finding is not a set of finds!

More frequently though, "-ing" added to the root of a verb is used as a verb or an adjective. For a thorough, hands-on discussion of these uses, refer to https://dictionary.cambridge.org/fr/grammaire/grammaire-britannique/verb-patterns-verb-infinitive-or-verb-ing. Here is an example:

"The apparatus was running all through the night"

(past continuous tense of the verb "run": past tense of to be (i.e., was) plus the verb's present participle (-ing word)). Another way of saying this would be:

"The apparatus ran all through the night"

eliminating the need for using the past continuous tense of the verb. By the way, we hope you noticed the use of the -ing form "saying" in the previous sentence: after all prepositions, an "-ing" form (gerund) is to be used, not an infinitive!

The gerund is sometimes used to replace the infinitive of the verb. For example, in this sentence:

*Déposer les deux vis de fixation de la trappe de l'ensemble filtre*

which was machine translated in a document we worked on as:

"Remove the two screws to fasten the filter assembly hatch"

the infinitive "to fasten" was used to indicate the fastening of the metal filter. But as read, the sentence means "Remove the two screws in order to fasten the metal filter", which is the exact opposite of what should be said. The correct translation is:

"Remove the two screws fastening the filter assembly hatch".

Replacing the infinitive "to fasten" by the gerund "fastening" makes the sentence both understandable, correct and smooth-flowing. The two screws are used to attach on the filter assembly hatch and have to be removed. (Note that this could also be translated as: "Remove the two screws used to fasten the filter assembly hatch.")

## 1.2.7 *Adjectives*

One of the difficulties that arises when writing in or translating into English is the placement of adjectives where these are placed before the noun in English, while, in French for example, they are more often placed after the noun (there are actually rules, even in French, believe it or not!). It is often very difficult to decide to which nouns the adjectives apply when there is more than one noun but only one adjective. This is a particular problem if machine translation is used, as a computer typically cannot follow this. An example that we found recently was a machine translation of the phrase:

> *Contre-indication pour l'utilisation (nouveaux nés, porteurs de pacemakers, les femmes enceintes et épileptiques)*

which was translated as:

> "Contraindications for use (newborns, pacemaker carriers, pregnant and epileptic women)".

There is a first mistake in that, in English, one refers to "pacemaker wearers" and not "pacemaker carriers". Neither is particularly obvious since really one is speaking of someone who has had a pacemaker implanted in their body, and not someone who is carrying it in their hand or wearing it like a scarf. This is not the real problem here. The correct phrase should be:

> "Contraindications for use (newborns, pacemaker carriers, pregnant women, and epileptics)".

The adjective *enceintes* ("pregnant") applies of course to the "women" while the word *épileptiques* is NOT an adjective here but a noun, meaning epileptic persons, though the word "person" is not needed here. Note also that while the adjectives in this French phrase must carry the "s" at the end as the nouns are plural, this is not the case in English, where adjectives are singular words. There are also no "feminine" versions of adjectives in English even though the word itself may be feminine. For example:

*hommes intelligents/femmes intelligentes*

is just

"intelligent men/intelligent women"

in English.

## 1.2.8 Adverbs

We said in the introduction to this book that we shall not be giving grammar lessons, but here is a subject that is really quite complicated: where do you place the adverb with respect to the verb? The problem is that there are different interpretations as to how this should be done. We checked out one website https://site.uit.no/english/grammar/adverb-placement/ and got some good tips, but this is from a university in Norway and written by someone of another nationality. We do not say they are wrong and you could take good lessons from the website, but there could be other interpretations that would be equally correct. For example, one statement on that website is that adverbs always come after the "be" verb (is, was, are, etc.). This means

"is always"

and not

"always is"

in the sense that

"Lead is always poisonous"

and not

"Lead always is poisonous".

However, if you check out the site https://textranch.com/156977/she-is-always/or/she-always-is/, you will find that statistically the before and after placements are about equal. But if you check out https://forum.wordreference.com/threads/en-there-always-is-there-is-always-adverb-placement.2169456/, you will see explanations as to why "is always" is correct while "always is" is an exception.

A native English speaker should know what is right, what does not sound right, and what is just wrong, though this is not guaranteed, so it is best to ask someone if in doubt. Or check out the various Internet sites giving grammar lessons, but if in doubt, try entering your phrase into an Internet search and see if it is used that way or another way.

If everything fails, try a reliable source (and we trust that you know how to choose the right ones): https://dictionary.cambridge.org/grammar/british-grammar/adverbs-and-adverb-phrases-position.

### 1.2.9 *Prepositions*

These are words that are used to express relationships between words. There is a vast array of prepositions, and the reader might like to check out some of the websites that discuss this topic (https://dictionary.cambridge.org/grammar/british-grammar/prepositions, https://7esl.com/list-of-prepositions/). Again, our intention is not to give a grammar lesson, but rather to point out some of the more common errors that we have seen appear in texts that we have proofread. Thus, we have given these in the non-exhaustive Table 1. It has to be said that these are things that you must learn by heart and the rules are not always strict. A native English speaker should know what sounds right

**Table 1.** Common errors in preposition usage.

| Incorrect English | Correct English | Incorrect Example | Correct Example |
|---|---|---|---|
| Compare **to** | Compare **with** | We compare our data **to** other data obtained using a different method. | We compare our data **with** other data obtained using a different method. |
| Compared **with** | Compared **to** | Compared **with** other methods, ours works better. | Compared **to** other methods, ours works better. |
| Independent **from** | Independent **of** | The variable x is independent **from** the other variables in the series. | The variable x is independent **of** the other variables in the series. |
| Composed **by** | Composed **of** | The mixture is composed **by** a number of different chemicals. | The mixture is composed **of** a number of different chemicals. |
| Associated **to** | Associated **with** | Associated **to** other results | Associated **with** other results |
| Belongs **with** | Belongs **to** | The data belongs **with** a set of environmental data. | The data belongs **to** a set of environmental data. |
| Consists **to** | Consists **of** | The experimental methods consists **to** first mixing the reagents. | The experimental methods consists **of** first mixing the reagents. |
| Compliance **to** | Compliance **with** | The equipment is in compliance **to** the specifications. | The equipment is in compliance **with** the specifications. |
| Proportional **with** | Proportional **to** | The density is inversely proportional **with** the volume. | The density is inversely proportional **to** the volume. |
| Lower **as** | Lower **than** | found to be much lower **as** expected[3] | found to be much lower **than** expected |
| Example where preposition is not needed | | Notify **to** a supplier | Notify a supplier |

---

[3] In fact this means exactly the opposite to what is intended in this phrase.

and what does not sound right. They will understand what you are trying to say but know that the grammar is incorrect. The problem arises, for example, because often the preposition used in English is quite different from that used in French and other languages. We shall not give the French versions, but you can probably recognise them. In addition, sometimes there are prepositions in French that you do not need in English. We shall give examples of these as well.

### 1.2.10 Words used incorrectly

This section addresses a few words which are *faux-amis* in many (but not all) contexts. We shall start with a classic (which is also a total false friend!).

#### "Realise"/*Réaliser*

In English, "realise" means coming to the understanding of something:

> "I realise that I have to go to the dentist today so I cannot go for coffee"
> "He realised that he was in the wrong when he said that".

In French, this word has a much wider meaning and it is common to see a French person write something like:

> *The experiment was realised*
> *The realisation of the object is done by machining.*

These sentences are completely wrong in English and should read, respectively:

> "The experiment was performed"
> "The production of the object is done by machining".

But that doesn't sound quite right. Let's try:

> "The creation of the object is done by machining".

Too fancy!

"The manufacture of the object is done by machining".

Too formal! OK, what about:

"The object is produced by machining".

Yes, that is good but you see, we have had to restructure the sentence to make it sound right. You see how lucky the French are to be able to use a word like "realise" or "realisation" in this context.[4]

## "Punctual"/*Ponctuel/lle*

As a professor in a French university, JBAM realised that when it came to attending meetings, his French colleagues were not very punctual. The meetings did not start on time. But the French have a word:

*Ponctuel* (m) / *Ponctuelle* (f)

that can mean other things as well. For example, a:

*visite ponctuelle*

is a "spot-check". The person whose work is checked does not know beforehand if and when the inspection is going to occur.

*Un opérateur doit vérifier le niveau de huile dans lé réservoir de façon* **ponctuelle**
"The operator must **occasionally** check the oil level in the tank"
*C'est un événement* **ponctuel**
"It is a **one-time** event".

Again, the French are lucky to have such a word that you know exactly what it means in context but how do you translate it in English? Certainly not as "punctual" in these latter examples.

---

[4] We should note that we were made aware that the word "realisation" is actually used quite extensively in mathematics though we would have thought that perhaps "production" was more suitable.

### "Control"/*Contrôle*

This is a great word and sometimes you can use it in English and sometimes not. So you can:

> "control the operation of a machine"
> "perform an operation of Quality Control"

but:

> *Contrôler une machine*

can literally mean that you:

> "control the operation of a machine"

or that you:

> "inspect the machine"

or

> "check the operation of the machine".

Usually, the word *contrôle* in French means to perform an "inspection" or a "check" (less formal). The word *commander* can mean "to control". The term:

> *système de commande et contrôle*

can be translated as

> "instrumentation and control system".[5]

Having said this, "controls" are performed on pharmaceutical products to check their quality and conformity.

---

[5] The words "Command and Control" are used in English in a military context.

## "Isolation"/*Isolation*

This is a word that can cause confusion as it can mean:

"insulation"

such as thermal or electrical insulation, or:

"isolation"

such as the electrical isolation of equipment or the mechanical isolation of a system. In other words, cutting off the electricity or the operation of a system.

One thing is certain and that is it should not be confused with:

"insolation"

which means:

"sunstroke"!

## Important/*Important*

In English, the word "important" means something that has great significance:

"An important event"
"An important career move"
"It is important that you pay your taxes on time".

It does NOT mean a lot of stuff. So to say:

"An important amount of data was collected"

is not correct. This implies that the data had some importance (for you, for science, etc.). You should rather say:

"A large amount of data was collected".

Similarly,

> "The most important radiation emission"

should be

> "The highest (or most intense) radiation emission"

and not the radiation emission that has the most significance. This term can be confusing if not properly translated (in context). For example:

> "The lab will have to establish operating procedures for handling important equipment".

Does that mean that the equipment has particular significance or that it is large, heavy, etc.? You will have to look at the context to be sure which interpretation to give.

## "On the contrary"/*Au contraire*

This is a phrase often seen in texts written by French-speaking authors. (We cannot speak for those of other nationalities). In fact, they are translating the phrase placed at the beginning of a sentence. For example:

> *D'habitude, une fonction d'onde réelle est propagée car V > E pour tous les canaux impliqués. Au contraire, pour la capture, on fait l'hypothèse que V < E.*

was translated as:

> "Usually, a real wave function is propagated as V > E.
> On the contrary, for capture, it is assumed that V < E."

The problem is that "on the contrary" is a very strong, aggressive statement. It is a negation of what has come before. A better thing to say is:

"Usually, a real wave function is propagated as V > E.
On the other hand, for capture, it is assumed that V < E."

This is much less aggressive and is just a gentle comparison. "On the one hand, this is done, on the other hand that is done".

While talking of hands, let us digress to briefly discuss another use of the word. Let's say we are discussing an equation:

$$A = B \text{ (where } B = C + D\text{)}.$$

If we want to discuss the term on the right of this equation, then we are talking about "B (where B = C + D)". No, we didn't mean that, we wanted to discuss the "B". OK, we could say:

"the right term".

But does that mean there is a "wrong term"? No, that is not what we mean. What we really should say is:

"the right-hand term"

or

"the right-hand side of the equation".

This is "B". "A" is the

"left-hand side of the equation".

Often these are abbreviated as "RHS" and "LHS".

If you are driving a car, you might want to be in the "left-hand lane" and you would be right (correct) as the "right" lane is the wrong lane for where you want to go.[6] (Note that "right" can also mean "completely" as in "turns right around"). So adding the word "hand" clarifies the meaning of "right" and hence "left". (Not to be "left" out!). To remember easily, "right/left" indicates a direction, while right-hand/left-hand indicates a position.

---

[6] The great American philosopher Yogi Berrah once said, "If you come to a fork in the road, take it!"

### 1.2.11 *Allow, enable, permit*

This particularly applies to European language speakers and the use of these verbs often gives a clear indication that the writer is not native English. English construction when using these verbs is completely different than in French, German, etc., and I have to say that speakers of these languages are very lucky in this respect. Let us give you an example. Very often you will see a phrase like:

> "which allows to control the wavelengths".

In this case it is a direct translation from French but it is not good English for you cannot use a structure like "allow", "enable", "permit" followed by an infinitive such as "to control". It is a great pity for it gives rise to all sorts of complications expressing this in English. In this case, the correct construction is:

> "which allows the wavelengths to be controlled".

You could say:

> "which allows us to control the wavelengths"

but then you speak in the active voice. You introduce yourself, or rather, your team. A digression — we cannot think of a case where in a scientific paper, you would use "I" speaking about yourself. You would always use "we", even if you actually do mean "I". We shall speak more later on about using plurals when referring to a single person.

Another example:

> "this operating mode does not allow to check the criteria for proper functioning"

which needs more work, thus:

> "this operating mode does not allow checking to be performed, of the criteria for proper functioning"

or should it be:

> "this operating mode does not allow checking of the criteria for proper functioning to be performed".

Here lies the problem. Both are correct, but the second version leaves the action too far along the sentence. So, choices have to be made. Again, one could say:

> "this allows us to check the criteria for proper functioning"

but we have introduced the active voice again and the paper starts to become "chatty". Like you are discussing it with a friend. A good scientific paper has to stand on its own merits and the active voice begins to bring in your personal opinion. This can be a trap, but it is up to the author to make this decision. As a general rule, if you do use the active voice, do not do it too often.

## 1.2.12 *"The" and "a"*

This is something that causes a lot of confusion because in French, for example, the definite article "the" (*le, la, les*) is used a great deal more than in English. There are 16 different types of "the" in German, while Slavic languages do not use articles at all. The clue to using them comes from their names:

- "The" is the definite article. It is used to identify a specific term or action.
- "A(n)" is the indefinite article.[7] It is used to identify a term or action in general.

A typical example of French overuse of "the" is given in this sentence:

---

[7] "An" is generally used before words beginning with vowels (a, e, i, o, u): e.g., "an apple", "an ear", "an ion", "an onion", "an underling", but also with words that sound as if they begin with a verb: e.g., "an hour". Some words beginning with vowels sound like consonants and so we have "a university", "a uniform". It just has to sound right.

"Participation in the commissioning of the apparatus,
in interface with **the** [Work Package 3]"

There is no need for "**the**". The apparatus has been definitely identified and it is redundant to add another "**the**". So the sentence should read:

"Participation in the commissioning of the apparatus,
in interface with [Work Package 3]".

On the other hand, we give an example of underuse, where English will insert "**the**" (We saw this while correcting a paper):

"Section Y presents the XYZ algorithm used for estimation of
relevant parameters".

This is a very general statement. It says that the XYZ algorithm can be used for estimation purposes of a general nature. Leaving out "the" before "estimation" makes the statement general. In this case, however, the full sentence said that the XYZ algorithm was used for getting information on the appropriateness of a particular statistical method. Thus, this was a specific application of the algorithm and so the sentence should have said:

"Section Y presents the XYZ algorithm used for **the** estimation of
relevant parameters".

The algorithm provides a means of obtaining information on this specific set of parameters. Another example where the use of "the" is needed is:

"kernels produced by rotating electrode process"

where "the" has simply been left out as if it does not exist. The correct phrase is:

"kernels produced by the rotating electrode process"

although one could also say:

> "kernels produced by rotating electrode processes".

In other words, changing the singular "process" into the plural "processes" renders the phrase more general (less definite). Thus, when you are talking about a specific (definite) object or process, you use "the"; if you talk in general terms you leave "the" out.

If you want to be vague about something (you are indefinite about it), you use "a":

> "**A** method of calculating wave functions is using **the** XXX method".

This is one possible way of doing the calculation. In contrast:

> "**The** method of calculating wave functions is using XXX".

This means that this is the way the calculation must be performed. A way of getting around the use of "a" is when you speak about plurals. So:

> "Ways of calculating wavefunctions are using XXX methods".

Here you can drop the "a".

We find that in French, writers of technical documentation sometimes do not use "the" when they should, and they sometimes use "a" when they mean "the". For example:

> "the signature of **an** oxidation of the particle"

does not make sense. It should read as:

> "the signature of **the** oxidation of the particle".

The oxidation that has occurred is a definite occurrence. If there was anything indefinite about the observation, one might say:

> "the signature of some sort of oxidation of the particle".

In summary, if in doubt, use the "definite/indefinite" criterion to see what you should be using.

### 1.2.13 *"In" and "into", "on" and "onto"*

A popular song in the 1960's had the title:

> "When you walk in the room".

You can check it out on Youtube.[8] Unfortunately, this is grammatically incorrect for it should really be:

> "When you walk into the room".

You walk or go:

> "into a room".

If you are already present there, you are:

> "in the room".

The word "into" is used along with an action verb. You:

> "enter into a discussion"
> "insert a needle into a septum"
> "pass an ion beam into the reaction chamber".

You may be:

> "involved in a discussion".

There may be:

> "liquid in the bottle"

---

[8] JBAM used to sing this when he was the singer of the famous rock group "Buster Proton and the Accelerators".

and

"the ion beam may collide with the target in the chamber".

What about "on" and "onto"? Again, "onto" is used along with action verbs:

"Place the sample onto the sample holder".

"On" is passive:

"The sample is on the sample holder".

You will find, however, that the use is less strict and if you say:

"Place the sample on the sample holder"

this is not incorrect in common usage. However, saying:

"The sample is onto the sample holder"

is very definitely incorrect.

## 1.2.14 *"This" and "that"*

"This" refers to something close by or close in time while "that" is for something more distant in place or time. We have noticed, however, when proofreading articles written by colleagues, that often they use the construction "the one". For example, when translating:

*différent de celui responsable*

referring to an organisation, they translate this as:

"different from the one responsible".

While understandable, this is awkward phrasing. A better interpretation is to use "that", referring to a person or thing not closely related. Thus:

"different from that responsible".

Another example from an article we proofread recently:

"the most famous being the Smith and Jones one".

Again, not incorrect but awkward. A better way to say this is:

"the most famous being that of Smith and Jones".

## 1.2.15 *"Of" and "off"*

We were asked by one of our colleagues to discuss the difference in these terms. Indeed, in English they are essentially pronounced the same and this could cause confusion for the author. Let's start with "of".

This is a preposition, used to express the origin of a word. Where it comes from or where it belongs, what the word refers to. Thus:

"The acceleration of gravity".

You would not say

"The gravity acceleration"

nor

"Gravity's acceleration".

Similarly,

"The first day of the month"
"The Prime Minister of Canada",

but you could say

"The Canadian Prime Minister".

Sometimes apostrophes are used instead of "of",[9] for example:

"Young's modulus"

and not

"The modulus of Young".

Often this is ruled by convention as in "The acceleration of gravity" above. However, apostrophes can sound clumsy when speaking, for example:

"The particle's velocity"

sounds wrong and it is better to say:

"The velocity of the particle".

And speaking of apostrophes, "of" is particularly useful when dealing with plurals. Thus, although you could say:

"The particles' velocity",

it is much better to say

"The velocity of the particles",

thus avoiding the plural apostrophe since when **speaking** it would not be clear if you were referring to one particle or more than one.[10]

Now what about "off"? Well, this is a completely different word, which can be an adverb, a preposition or an adjective (see, e.g., https://dictionary.cambridge.org/english/off). As an adverb and as

---

[9] Usually with names of people, animals, countries, etc. See Additional Reading section, "Practical English Usage" (Swan): 440.2.

[10] Oddly, translators don't seem to like the use of "of" and prefer, for example, "application date" rather than "date of application", "vehicle weight" rather than "weight of the vehicle", etc. Avoiding the "of" might perhaps seem more concise. This is really a debatable point that rather belongs in the second half of this book but in my opinion (JBAM), if the term without the "of" is not in common usage (for example: "term end" instead of "end of term"), then dropping the "of" is not valid.

a preposition, it means "away from a place or position, especially the present place, position, or time". Thus you:

"Turn off the lights" (adverb)
"This cheese tastes off" (adjective, meaning "not fresh")
"Fall off a bike" (preposition).

## 1.2.16 Gender-neutral text

If you know that Dr. Smith is a man and he did something, you can use "he".

"He did such and such".

The same applies to Dr. Jones whom you know to be a woman.

"She developed the theory".

But suppose you don't know if Dr. Smith is a man or a woman. What do you do? Or let's say you are talking about a person in general that could be man or woman. In this case you could use:

"He/She"

but while this is OK, it is not very elegant and cannot at all be used for Dr. Smith or Dr. Jones. In languages that stress genders, this problem generally does not arise because there are often clues given by the gender of adjectives, verbs, etc. In English there are no such clues.

To solve this problem, we can resort to a convention which in itself is strange, counterintuitive and that requires quite a bit of skill to maintain consistency. We refer to the person (singular) in the plural. Thus:

"When Dr. Smith applied their theory, they quickly saw its inadequacies".

So we have a plural possessive adjective:

"their"

and not

> "his"

and a plural form of personal pronoun

> "they"

and not

> "he".

The same applies to a woman (Dr. Jones). We neutralise them by referring to them in the plural. Again:

> "If the operator wants to cool the reactor fast, they will drive in the control rods."

We cannot and never should assume that the operator will be a man. Very politically incorrect!

Now while we are talking about genders, we should mention a few rules and a couple of oddities. If we know we are referring to a woman, we say:

> "she did something",

and if it is a man,

> "he did something".

So English does have certain rules as to how we distinguish genders. Again, it may be safer to say:

> "they did something",

though you are referring to a single person. OK, so far, so good. But you must remember that you have used a plural pronoun and so the verbs going along with it must be in the plural form. Instead of:

> "He is going to perform the experiments"

you must say

> "They are going to do the experiments".

The problem is that things get complicated when there is more than one person involved. Let's take the sentence:

> "Dr. Jones was telling the students about the theory of quantum mechanics. They were fascinated about it".

Wait…who was fascinated, Dr. Jones (they) or the students (they)? How do you get around this one? Well, you have to be imaginative and try to make things as clear as possible. Maybe by repeating words. Thus:

> "Dr. Jones was telling the students about the theory of quantum mechanics. This is a subject that Dr. Jones is fascinated in".

Now people know which "they" you were referring to. We shall see later in the book, when we speak about translating patents, how this very subject is at the heart of patent writing, where you must be very specific about what or who does what. As a spoiler, in patent-speak we would say:

> "Dr. Jones was telling said students about the theory of quantum mechanics. Said Dr. Jones was fascinated about said quantum theory",

and in a patent, you never use personal pronouns anyway!

Before we leave genders, there is a twist that is very typically English. Normally objects are neutral in English so when referring to a piece of equipment, you would say:

> "it is an oscilloscope"

or

> "those are oscilloscopes that you see there".

But what if you are talking about a car? Cars are feminine!

> "She drives like a dream"

means that the car is very pleasant to drive. Similarly, ships are feminine. When launched, the standard phrase is:

> "God bless her and all who sail in her".

We think airplanes are also probably feminine, but we are not sure. In any case, you can also just say

> "it is a dream to drive".

### 1.2.17 Numbers

Make sure that when you quote a number that has a decimal point, you use "." and not ",". Thus:

$$25.932$$

and not

$$25,932.$$

This is very important as 25,932 means 25 thousand, nine hundred and thirty-two! In English, the numbers to the left of the decimal point are separated by commas. Thus:

$$10,943,247.462$$

is 10 million, 943 thousand, two hundred and forty-seven POINT four six two. Note that when speaking in English, after the decimal point the individual digits are pronounced (NOT point four hundred and sixty-two, as would be said in French).

We shall give Table 2 more for information than for useful purpose as in scientific articles, the American terminology is used rather than the "old" British system. (The latter is no longer used in official documents in the UK but people sometimes do talk of million million).

### 1.2.18 Punctuation

Punctuation is very important when writing and we have noticed that many French people do not use enough punctuation when

**Table 2.** American and British terminology for scientific numbers.

| Number (Scientific) | US Term (Système Internationale) | UK Term | Prefix |
|---|---|---|---|
| $10^6$ | Million | Million | Mega- |
| $10^9$ | Billion | Thousand Million | Giga- |
| $10^{12}$ | Trillion | Billion | Tera- |
| $10^{15}$ | Quadrillion | Thousand Billion | Peta- |
| $10^{18}$ | Quintillion | Trillion | Exa- |

constructing sentences. For example, take this sentence (taken from a paper written in English by a French native speaker):

> "Concerning the properties of the mathematical tools we propose when the hypothesis XXX is violated, the following result arises".

Without the punctuation, this means that:

> "the proposed tools yield the following result when the hypothesis is violated".

In fact, this was not at all the meaning of this sentence. It should have had a comma between "tools" and "we"; hence:

> "Concerning the properties of the mathematical tools, we propose **that** when the hypothesis XXX is violated, the following result arises".

(We also have inserted "that" to be more correct).

Another quirk that we find in French is that sometimes a comma (",") is used in the middle of a sentence where an English person would have placed a "full-stop" ("period" in US English) or a semi-colon (";") or even the word "and":

> "Scanning Electron Microscopy was performed using the Gentle Beam mode (GB), this method decelerates incident electrons…"

There is clearly a break here and in fact this should be written as:

> "Scanning Electron Microscopy was performed using the Gentle Beam mode. This method decelerates incident electrons…"

The comma just does not make sense in this example. Another example is:

> "The input data will come from Work Package 2 for the mechanical assembly, the electrical installation is also handled by Work Package 2"

which should be replaced by:

> "The input data will come from Work Package 2 for the mechanical assembly. The electrical installation is also handled by Work Package 2"

or by

> "The input data will come from Work Package 2 for the mechanical assembly and the electrical installation is also handled by Work Package 2".

If we consider the sentence:

> "Some grades of steel cannot be treated in a vacuum the resulting loss of nitrogen would result in an unacceptable increase in ferrite content".

Again, there is a break that is awkward. The explanation for the first part does not follow naturally. We can make this smoother by adding "as", thus:

> "Some grades of steel cannot be treated in a vacuum as the resulting loss of nitrogen would result in an unacceptable increase in ferrite content".

An example of the use of a semi-colon is:

> "Fuel rods are filled with uranium dioxide pellets compressed by a spring; they may contain other components such as a spacer and a pellet of alumina".

The colon ":" is a very useful punctuation mark when starting a list. For example:

> "The following equipment is needed: a stopwatch, glass beaker, Bunsen burner, thermometer and a stirring rod".

Note the use of "a" in this sentence. It is not necessary to keep repeating it but the final "a" rounds off the list. The rule is actually to repeat "a" or "the" everywhere, which rapidly becomes heavy, or just for the first and last item of an enumeration.

If in doubt, use more punctuation marks if it helps to clarify the sentence. Try reading the sentence over to yourself and see where the breaks in continuity are. Read it out loud. This will help you place them.

## 1.2.19 *Phrasing (word order)*

This is a subject that deserves mentioning and requires careful execution if it is done. Let us look at the following sentence:

> "By means of its base plate, the means of attachment of which will be defined with the supplier of the [Work Package 2], the device will be fixed on the frame".

This sounds very clumsy to a native English speaker. The sentence (modified for proprietary reasons) came from a machine translation of a call for tender. We shall speak more about the hazards of machine translation later, but in fact this is a fairly accurate interpretation of the original French sentence. The problem is the ordering of the phrases. Thus, it would be better to be reconstructed as follows:

"The device will be fixed onto the frame, by means of its base plate the attachment of which will be defined along with the supplier".

The main subject of the sentence "The device will be fixed onto the frame" is placed at the beginning of the sentence instead of being relegated to the end, as if it did not matter. Think about this if you construct a complex sentence like this but be careful as there is the chance that the meaning could be mixed up in doing so. If in doubt, pass it by an English-speaking colleague to see what they think. A clue to how the sentence should sound can be found by the fact that usually, one less comma will be needed — though this is not a strict rule.

Another example of phrasing where things become mixed up and unclear is this sentence:

*Une photo est jointe en annexe du test.*

Literal translation:

"A photo is attached in the appendix of the test".

This literally means that the "photo is attached in the test's appendix". Or does the sentence mean:

"A photo of the test is given in the appendix"

(this appendix being part of the document where the sentence occurs)? This is not clear. Phrasing is extremely important so that the actual meaning is properly transmitted. You should always re-read your sentences with this concept in mind to ensure that you have not mixed up subjects, objects and intentions.

### 1.2.20 *Sentence style*

As we have said earlier in this book, we have written it from a conversational point of view. Our goal has been to speak directly to you as the reader and so we may have used shortened words like "don't", we have started sentences with "But", etc., all the things we have said not to do when writing a scientific article. The purpose of a scientific article is to present facts, not to try to convince the user that its content is correct, or important to them. That is for the reader to decide, being appraised of the facts presented therein. So scientific style is primarily based on accuracy, clarity and, ideally, readability. This does not mean that it has to be written so that everyone can understand it. That is the role of the popular press. A scientific article has a certain targeted audience who should understand the concepts presented so that they can take in this knowledge and access its authenticity. At the same time, concepts that are perhaps less than familiar, even to the expert, should be properly explained.

It is not necessary that it be written in a very literary style and the rules learned in a creative writing class do not apply. In particular, terms should be used consistently throughout the body of the article. It is said that the Inuit have 50 different words for snow. This idea should not be applied when writing a technical article. If a term is used once, use the same term every time. This may result in rather dull writing but at least the reader will constantly know what you are talking about.

A couple of JBAM's favourite authors are Marcel Proust and James Joyce. The former is famous for his page-long sentences while in the Molly Bloom soliloquy, there are pages and pages of text without the benefit of punctuation. This may leave an impression of genius on the reader of these works but do not try this at home (as they say). Try to keep sentences as short as possible without giving up the free flow of the text. A sentence that stretches on and on can quickly leave the reader feeling lost and may end up with them completely misunderstanding what you wanted to say. So in practice, read through your text and see if you can reduce the length of sentences while still maintaining an even flow. As with any written work, it is always a good idea to pass it by a knowledgeable colleague to see if they understand it. If they point out inconsistencies or vague concepts, it will provide you with the ideal opportunity to correct these, before the reviewer gets their hands on the paper!

So, be concise and clear. A wonderful guide that follows its own recommendations (44 pages long) is "The Elements of Style" by William Strunk. Since its original edition of 1920, it did not wrinkle a bit (as they say in French!).

### 1.2.21 *Machine translation*

Machine translation is becoming impossible to avoid. People trust computers. People trust what they do not understand. Machine translation works well on simple sentences with elementary grammar.

"George eats an apple"

will most certainly be correctly translated in French as

*Georges mange une pomme*

(and *vice versa*). But try

"We take one mole of salt".

If you are lucky, you will get:

*Nous prenons une mole de sel,*

which is correct. But you could get, with almost equal probability:

*Nous prenons **un grain de beauté** (i.e., a mole) de sel*

or

*Nous prenons **une taupe** (i.e., a mole) de sel.*

(JBAM) I have often been asked to correct the English in someone's paper and generally it is clear what the person wanted to say. But then you find that the person has used machine translation to do a quick and dirty job. Here is a phrase I came across in a student's paper they had prepared for a conference:

> "The electrical contacts group in reindeer has been active for many years".

What the…? Oh yes, of course. They were talking about the electrical contacts group in "Rennes". The capital of the Brittany region in France. But in French *Rennes* means "reindeers". The computer had never heard of Rennes so how was it to know what a beautiful town it is. This is just one isolated example, but in this case, as I continued reading the article, I just had no clue what the student wanted to say as it was so garbled by this automatic translation. Eventually I threw it back to them and told them NEVER to use machine translation again.

Another example we came across recently was in a text dealing with mechanical "actuators" and the phrase:

> *S'assurer du changement d'état des actionneurs suivants*

was automatically translated as:

> "Ensure that the status of the following shareholders changes".

A "shareholder" in a financial sense being called an *actionneur* in French. You should remember that machine translation, if not specifically targeted to a given context, just loves *faux-amis*.

There are circumstances where machine translation can actually do a not-so-bad job. For example, law texts often use the same phrase as do technical manuals. If sophisticated machine translation programs using deep learning are applied to repetitive or semi-repetitive text, then the outcome can be quite surprising. But this is the domain of the professional translator and when checking the text, this is no longer proofreading but post-editing. That is, you have to read the text, understand the context, and possibly re-write it to correct grammar and meaning. Often the same word, repeated many times in a text, is translated differently each time it appears, sometimes with ludicrous consequences.

We shall discuss machine translation in more detail later in Section 3.4 in the context of professional translation. In fact, this has become more and more pervasive in the profession, but it should be done by technicians skilled in the procedure, using software that incorporates "deep learning" (the current-day term for Artificial Intelligence at work) and not by someone who wants to get a quick and dirty translation that will be cleaned up later by a helpful colleague.

Bottom line is, if you are writing an original scientific article, do NOT use machine translation. It will only give your friendly native much grief.

## 1.3 Final Word

For some people reading this, sitting down and writing an article in a foreign language poses no problems. You can think and rationalise clearly and you can get your point across as you wish to do. For others, this is not so simple, and your ability to put forward your ideas and to explain what you have done and achieved are muted by your inherent language limitations. This is a serious handicap and can have a deleterious effect on your scientific production. Our advice for this is quite simple. Write the article in your native tongue and make sure that you say all you wish to say. Explain your science as you see it. Now you have two choices:

a) Have a go at translating it yourself and then find someone able to do a good proofreading job
b) Hire a translator to do the job for you.

Publishing in some journals such as *Phys. Rev.* or *J. Chem. Phys.* involves onerous page charges which may be worth it to get your paper into a prestigious review. Open-source publishing also comes with a hefty price. In other words, it costs money to publish. Why not make the investment to make sure that your article:

a) Is accurate and clearly explains your work
b) Will pass by the reviewers without the ominous "The paper is sound but the English needs extensive rework".

## 1.4 Feedback (rex) from non-French-speaking Colleagues

Professor Mats Larsson, Stockholm University, Sweden:

"From my (Swedish) perspective, the -ing form is difficult. It can be a participle, gerund or preposition. Gerund we hardly use in Swedish, and often the participle is dangling in scientific texts.

I also find the indefinite article "a" difficult. Sometimes one should use it, sometimes not, and I don't have a good ear for when to use it.

I have used "The Chemist's English" by Robert Schoenfeld for many years and found it very useful. Fowler's "Modern English Usage" is also on my bookshelf."

Professor Eli Jerby, Tel-Aviv University, Israel:

"In our seemingly global era, the differences between cultures are yet reflected in languages and dialects (and even in various expression styles in the same language).

Translation is probably not just a matter of lingual conversion, but more like a transformation of one way of thinking and perception to another. It actually requires a re-writing (and reconstruction) of the message rather than just a substitute of words and sentences. In this respect, scientific translation may encounter similar challenges to poetry translation."

Professor Minna Patenen, University of Oulu, Finland:

"There are several peculiarities in Finnish that are causing problems for me when writing English (or French). Or I would rather say that English has peculiarities and we have things simpler in Finnish! For example, we do not use articles (a/an/the), so when I am writing a text in English, I usually omit 90% of them in the first round and then add them in the next round. I hope I am getting better, but I really have trouble understanding what are "abstract" things which do not need an article (e.g., "Resolution is defined by the width of an entrance slit and a pass energy. The resolution of the used instrument was 0.1 eV.") I would not write "a" resolution to the first one, but then I would have "the resolution" but I have no idea if it is correct.)

*(Continued)*

*(Continued)*

> I have also wondered if the lack of future tense in Finnish causes confusion sometimes when I write e-mails in English, since I might write that "I do something" instead of "I will do something".
>
> Punctuation rules seem to be very different in these two languages, so I might have a proper amount of commas in my text but in wrong places. In Finnish, we place comma in front of conjunctions but, that, since, while, whereas, when, if, until, because, so.
>
> One part that I will read extra carefully is the section about "allow, enable, permit". Allow and enable do not really translate directly in Finnish, or they sort of do but then the sentence sounds very formal in Finnish. I use them in my writing but probably wrongly.
>
> The verb "to benefit" is my boss' favourite word. He puts it everywhere in a sense that "the experiment will benefit from high degree of coherence of the X-ray beam" which I think is ok, but he can also write "High degree of coherence will be benefitted". Is this correct? For me it sounds like a sort of direct translation from Finnish and probably not ok."

Professor Lars Andersen, University of Aarhus, Denmark:

> "The only Danish peculiarity I can think of is that we are allowed to put words together in one word like 'sygehusdirektør' = 'hospital director' or 'afdelingssygeplejerske' = 'department nurse'. This can actually construct some very long words. A difficulty that I have faced is related to: how to put three words or more together. Examples: Single-count detector, laser-beam focus (I guess this is the correct way of doing it?)."

Dr. Michael Sztucki, European Synchrotron Radiation Facility (ESRF), Grenoble, France:

> "Some thoughts I had concerning me as a German native speaker: In German, we are used to constructing very long (and complicated) sentences. You know, many clauses, commas, and the verb at the very end of the phrase :-) In scientific articles, you should construct short and clear sentences with structure S-V-O. The problem for me was how to do this best without always using the same structure, which risks making the article more boring to read. How to advance some parts of the phrase, how to use commas in this case, etc."

(*Continued*)

Dr. Octavio Roncero, Instituto de Fisica Fundamental, Madrid, Spain and Dr. André Canosa, Université de Rennes I, Rennes, France:

When we contacted him, Dr. Roncero provided us with a "raw" article that was in the process of being prepared for publication so that we could assess the English. Indeed, problems that we saw were very similar to those of French authors and these have been discussed in the different sections above. There were some things, however, that caught our eye and these were spelling errors such as "accesible" instead of "accessible". In fact, André Canosa explained to us that the "s" in Spain is hard and that "ss" is not used. Thus, his name is pronounced like "Canoza" in France but like "Canossa" in Spain. As stated in Section 1.2.6 regarding the missing "s" at the end of plurals, when doing direct authoring you may hear the text in your mind but it can be affected by your accent and way of speaking.

# Chapter 2

# Reviewing

## 2.1 Introduction

As a scientist, when you get known in your field, you will often be asked to review the work of others. This is an unpaid duty if you like but it has its merits and you do it because you hope that someone will do the same for you when you decide to publish. Like Yogi Berra said:

> "You should always go to people's funerals, or they will not come to yours."

(This is really worth an Internet search!).

(JBAM) has been a reviewer for many scientific journals in different fields (over 70 *Physical Review A* and *Physical Review Letters* articles, articles for *Journal of Physics B: Atomic, Molecular and Optical Physics, Journal of Chemical Physics, Physical Chemistry-Chemical Physics, Combustion and Flame, Plasma Sources, Science and Technology*, etc). Reviewing is an excellent way of keeping abreast of developments in the field and also of participating in the improvement of authors' papers. It is a confidential job by its very nature and JBAM has often been very grateful to anonymous reviewers of his papers who have seen things that were missed, areas of improvement and clarification, and pointed out errors that he was not aware of. (Not that this has happened often of course!). Indeed, it is much better if a reviewer finds your mistake before the article gets published and forever sits in a library hiding this *faux-pas*! Reviewing requires a lot of concentration and it is essential that you have at least a general understanding of the content of the paper. So, it is also an opportunity for you to improve your culture, not just scientifically, but linguistically as well. If you want to become proficient in a language, it is essential to read in that language and so here is a perfect way to acquire new skills, in particular in the context of the field in which you work.

The journal *Nature* is especially famous for its high rejection rate of articles and, being aware of this, has published a number of articles on this subject. Some interesting articles concerning how to appeal reviews and on the general subject of reviewing come from *Nature Immunology* and *Nature Cell Biology*. These are open-source articles so you can find them on the Internet even if you do not have access to the whole journal:

- *Nature Immunology* **volume 8**, page 541 (2007)
- *Nature Cell Biology* **volume 13**, page 109 (2011)

Reviewing requires a lot of discretion, especially when writing a negative review or at least one where you suggest that more work has to be done before an article can be published. The last thing that one should set out to do is to insult the authors and indeed we have never come across a case where that has occurred, although obviously this is a personal opinion. There are some fields, however, where the financial stakes are very high and there is a lot of competition for funding, thus one might be tempted to denigrate the authors who happen to be competitors. This is a scurrilous practice that does sometimes occur.

This is not, however, the thrust of this particular section. What we want to explain is how to avoid unintentionally causing offence. If the reference is not in your native language, this could perhaps occur.

## 2.2 Misunderstandings

We recently reviewed a reference letter submitted by a colleague, who was rejecting a paper on academic grounds but wanted to make sure that the language he had used was accurate. He was not a native English speaker and neither were the authors of this particular paper. In one sentence, the reviewer said:

> "there were too many "useless" details".

While this may indeed have been correct, the word "useless" is very strong and perhaps a bit insulting. We recommended that this be changed to:

> "there were too many details that were not very useful".

This softens the tone and allows the author to reflect on whether this statement is helpful. To say that something is "useless" is very final and can put the author into a combative mood for the response.

Another example like this is to say that something is:

> "irrelevant".

Maybe in context it can appear harmless but probably it is better to say:

> "not relevant",

though often this could be replaced with:

> "not applicable",

usually abbreviated as NA or N/A.

Another phrase that was used in this review was when the reviewer referred to the submitted articles as:

> "a piece of work".

However, "a piece of work" in English can also mean something quite different. Something reprehensible. To say that someone or something is "a piece of work" is really quite an insult. This was not in any way what the reviewer wanted to say, and probably the authors would not have understood this significance of this phrase, but still we recommended that it be changed to just:

"this article".

A very good French friend and colleague is often asked to review articles that come from foreign authors and frequently he has to criticise the English in the text. He is embarrassed to make such a criticism in a referee report in which he himself might make some English errors so he always asks us to check it before he sends it off. Not a bad idea!

When JBAM first moved to France, he often came across instances where what he wanted to say caused people to "snigger", i.e., to laugh in an embarrassed way. For example, when mentioning his throat (*mon cou*), people heard him as saying *mon cul* which means "my arse"! (But this word (as incorrectly pronounced) is a terrible one as there are other meanings even more embarrassing if you don't pronounce it exactly right!).

This is an area where there are a lot of traps, so unintentional misunderstandings can occur. On one occasion, one of our friends and colleagues sent an e-mail where they were reminding us that we had not returned a document and said:

"Could you kindly send me it as soon as possible".

In fact, they were being nice, but to say

"Will you KINDLY do something"

means:

"You have NOT done this and would you get a move on and DO IT!"

Again, that was not what our friend meant at all.

If you are in any doubt, have a native speaker do a quick check on your report. It might save you a lot of embarrassment. You might notice that senior politicians often use interpreters in interviews with foreigners, even though they might speak their language quite well, for an ill-expressed phrase might have an unintended meaning that could have serious consequences.

# Chapter 3

# Technical Translation for Translators

## 3.1 Introduction

In this chapter, we shall discuss the field of technical translation as practiced by professional translators. This is a very wide subject covering many specialty areas (Mechanical, Civil, Nuclear, Chemical Engineering, Transport, Pharmaceuticals, Electricity and Electronic Industries, etc.). We shall discuss many of these in subsequent chapters but let's start by saying what we shall not deal with. There is a saying in English: "Jack of all trades and master of none". When setting out to work as a technical translator you need to know your limits, and this is not always obvious. If you are asked to do a translation on a subject you know nothing about, you will probably make a mess of it. The client will not be happy and will quickly let you know.

1. At best this is embarrassing.
2. At worst — You might not get paid!
3. At very worst: Your translation could lead to accidents!

Having the right terminology is not enough. Far from it. Overconfidence is your worst enemy. Stick to the field where you have inside knowledge. If you do not know the context, the machine they are used in, and you cannot be in direct contact with the client, think first before taking the job.

Ultimately, technical translation is not about words but about the meaning of words (definition, concepts and content). Many fields have very specialised vocabulary, and you need to either know this or have access to it, but most importantly you need to understand it. Just "cherry-picking" in a dictionary — choosing a word from a list of possibilities — can be disastrous. This is where your personal knowledge comes in. For example, neither of the authors have had medical training so in this book we shall not discuss medical translation.

Point 3 could all too easily become a reality here. That being said, we have done translations concerning medical equipment. A memorable one was for the catalogue of a manufacturer of surgical instruments used in ophthalmology. Fortunately, the client provided a glossary, so this filled in the gaps in our knowledge.

Another field that is rather impenetrable is the textile industry. Its vocabulary goes back centuries, and woe betide any novice from putting a toe into its perimeter, unless of course you happen to come across a very good, illustrated dictionary. The same applies to all manufacturing fields with a long tradition behind them (e.g., printing and metallurgy). Fields that have developed over centuries, often locally in one language, where there was no thought of translation. You have to know exactly what the "thing" or procedure is you are translating. Just words will not help and you will never have time to read a textbook on a given craft.[1]

We shall come back to this aspect in a later chapter. Bottom line is, if you do not feel comfortable, politely refuse the job. Nobody wants a botch-up, so they will understand.

Many people whom you encounter in the translation industry have received training in translation or linguistics but inevitably in an Arts environment. This is especially true when dealing with translation agencies (more about those later) and many would-be technical

---

[1] By the way, French has the wonderful, all-encompassing word *métier* (a likely crossover word between "servant" and "mystery"), which you should carefully translate as "craft", "profession", even "department", but seldom "trade" (which is what Google recommends).

translators do not know one end of a torque wrench from another. Still, they are skilled at putting a sentence together.[2]

A good technical translator understands what they are translating. This does not necessarily mean that if you have a degree in laser physics, you cannot do a translation on let's say a construction project. A scientific training first of all makes you think, and thinking is not an obvious faculty. Nor natural, as a matter of fact. Our brain likes to stay in a low-consumption mode. We cannot emphasise this enough: you have to understand what you are translating (and/or post-editing), otherwise mistakes slip in. Many professions involve following a protocol or doing well what you have been taught to do. Scientists are out in the wilderness trying to find answers and you have to be able to understand the problem and how and where to search for the answers. This is the fun part of technical translation. You see a word and you have to find out how on earth you would say that in whatever language you are translating into. We shall give examples of this later. It really helps to have a wide knowledge as well so that you can, for example, understand what a machine does and how it will operate. To be able to imagine in your mind what the object described actually looks like. How a process or a test will actually be conducted. Science is a field that requires constant learning so bear this in mind. Read as many well-written articles as possible in different magazines and books in the fields you are going to work in. Get to know what is happening in the world. The monthly magazines of the learned societies (like *Physics Today*, *Physics World*, *Chemistry Today*, *Chemical & Engineering News*, etc.) are great ways to keep up with what is happening in the world of Physics and Chemistry, for example. Another surprising magazine that is a wealth of information is *The Economist* that each week carries the news of what is exciting and new in science as well as being one of the few reliable sources in the world on international business and politics. Well worth the price of a subscription.

---

[2] We must confess one of our limitations. Neither of the authors have much of a clue as to how to translate marketing material. This is not just word-for-word translation; it involves a complete re-write and you have to have the experience of "how would you say that in English". Leave this to those that are knowledgeable in this field.

We learned all that we needed to know about the structure and action of the Covid-19 virus from reading a major review in this magazine in March 2020!

In the following we shall give you tips on what you need to have to be a technical translator. What are the tools of the trade? We shall also discuss individual subjects and how to tackle them and to find the information you need to produce a document you can have confidence in.

Most of the translation work that the authors of this book do is for so-called translation agencies. These are businesses who find and deal directly with clients and who assign translation jobs in the appropriate languages to their hand-picked translators. Often this process begins, for a translator who is new to the agency, by a test translation that is submitted in order to show the translator's skill and appropriateness for the type of translation that is asked.[3]

It is difficult to imagine how translation was done before the advent of computers. It must have taken forever to type out text as you read the document you were translating, looking from the book to the typewriter keyboard. Checking and proofreading must have been a nightmare never to speak of how to make corrections. "Liquid paper" (a kind of quick drying white paint) was always at hand to erase the offending word and then positioning the print head over the dry white mark was always tricky. The invention of word processors like Word, WordPerfect and others went a long way to making the writer's life easier and more organised.

One of us (JBAM) can remember, when as a postdoc in Canada, his Professor coming back from a visit to the University of Berkeley in California with an exciting find. A machine that did word processing! You typed on a keyboard and what you typed appeared on a screen. The professor's secretary was horrified as her IBM Selectric typewriter was dear to her heart. It was a real struggle taking this away

---

[3] Be careful when agreeing to do tests. Some of them can be scams where the test is actually the job to be done. A test that involves translating more than a couple of hundred words could be suspicious. A good agency will offer to pay for the test but if you have worked for them before, this may not be a criterion.

from her and forcing her to use this electronic contraption. This machine didn't last long though, as the development of the Personal Computer and the accompanying software took over to the point where anyone could have easy access to this most remarkable of tools. Electronic editing.

## 3.2 Tools of the Trade

What do you need in order to do scientific or technical translations? What resources must you invest in? The first one is obvious: you need a computer. One you are comfortable with and that has enough dynamic memory (at least 8 Gb) that you will need when using the Computer Aided Translation tools we shall talk about in Section 3.3.

A computer alone is not enough for you will also need a good, fast and reliable Internet connection. These days almost all work come to you via the Internet. You will also spend a lot of time searching and there are fields where you will see many images before finding the right term. Again, it is difficult to imagine how translators operated before the invention of this marvel.

You must have a printer and a scanner. Some people are very happy working exclusively from a screen but the ability to print out some text, maybe to look at the layout you will have to achieve, is a big benefit. Colour printers are very inexpensive and colour cartridges very expensive. Essentially the actual machines are giveaways. The companies make their money from the consumables. The best buy is a Black & White laser printer. The price of the toner cartridge is an eye-opener but they last for a long time and do not dry out, unlike ink cartridges. And they are fast. We have one each and they get plenty of action.

A scanner is also an essential tool as it is really a piece of office equipment, an accessory to the actual translating activity. If you have a business structure where you can deduct expenses, you need a scanner to produce copies of receipts that you pick up as you go along. Although our printers also function as scanners, we also have a standalone feedthrough scanner that is very compact and very fast.

If you do a lot of work, you can easily fill up your computer's hard disk so a backup disk is a good solution here. You should also think about backing up your work in case of calamities happening, like a computer that decides not to turn on. One of us (JBAM) views computers as consumables, replacing them when they break down. This view is not shared by AIFM. Of course, USB keys are always a necessity for transferring files.

Some years ago, we attended a conference for translators and were looking forward to a particular presentation from the owner of a translation agency. We were hoping to get information about how to contact them, how to get business from agencies, etc. Imagine our surprise when the speaker gave a presentation on how to avoid work-related injuries. And this applied to translators!

As a translator, you are going to spend umpteen hours a day sitting on a chair in front of a computer screen and keyboard. The first thing you need is…comfort. You must be able to maintain a position without straining your back or your eyes and be able to avoid as many neck movements as possible. In retrospect, he was right. You have to look after yourself and try to avoid problems like carpal tunnel syndrome from using a mouse or a keyboard too much. This is a very individual topic but one worth bearing in mind. Think about the mouse that fits your hand better, the chair you are most comfortable in, the desk that is the right height, etc.

OK so now you are sitting comfortably in front of a nice computer screen with all your gear around you. You are ready to begin the task but where do you find your terminology? You have been given a job concerning the specifications for the renovation of a building and you don't recognise the terms you are seeing in front of you. What you need is a dictionary or a glossary. Your standard general dictionary (Larousse, Collins, Oxford, etc.) probably won't be of much help so you need to have the technical dictionaries that address specific subjects. We shall discuss these individually in Chapter 4 but if you are going to work on aeronautical translation, invest in an aeronautical dictionary. Be prepared to get the resources you need to do the job.

We have lots of dictionaries on our shelves, but it has to be said that it is much easier to have them in electronic form and if this is possible, get these. It is much quicker to do a "search" through an electronic file that fingering through page after page. This is not a hard-and-fast rule however, so if you can have both, so much the better.

### 3.2.1 *Spelling and grammar checkers*

One of the great advantages of electronic editing, whether using word processing software such as Word, WordPerfect, etc., or Computer Assisted Translation tools (discussed in the next section) is that they have in-built spelling and grammar checkers. This is wonderful and you can see right away if you have misspelled something or left out punctuation or plurals, etc. However, and there is always a "however", they are not foolproof because when you made that typing error, you may have created another word that actually exists. You wanted to write:

"ton"

but you wrote:

"tin".

The "I" and the "O" are side-by-side on the keyboard so it is very easy to make this mistake. But "tin" is a proper word so the spell-checker will not pick it up. Also be careful about grammar checkers as their suggestions are not always what you want to say.

It is ironic to say, although not surprising, that automatic spell-checkers and grammar checkers are still less reliable than human proofreaders. This is because you know (or the proofreader should know) what is meant to be said in the text, but the machine does not. Books today (maybe) contain less spelling errors, but more true errors than in the past! The bottom line here is that you must read your document. And better still, get someone else to read it. It is then easy to pick out errors when inappropriate words pop into your text, unannounced.

Much of what we have said in this section is rather obvious but has to be included for completeness. In the next section however, we shall deal with the essential tool of the technical translator and that is the Computer Aided Translation system. In the modern world this is indispensable, and you won't be able to get jobs without knowing how to use these programs. Don't worry, the most painful aspect is their price but an investment on them can pay enormous dividends.

## 3.3 Computer Aided Translation (CAT) Tools

Whether you are writing an original article in your own language and decide to translate it (or have it translated) or you are translating someone else's document, the most efficient and sure way to do this is by using the so-called Computer Aided Translation (CAT) tools. This is not to be confused with machine translation that we shall discuss in Section 3.4. What do these tools do and why are they so useful?

Basically, there are two or three major players in this field, these being Trados Studio, MemoQ and Wordfast. These are general use tools and are designed to help the translator do their job on any type of document. There are other, more specific tools such as Wordbee, Transifex, Crowdin, etc., that are used for company-specific work or for translating websites. Note that these lists are not exhaustive and other systems can also be offered for specific jobs.

The common denominator in this type of software is that the source language (the original text) is displayed in one column and the translator then enters the target language, i.e., the translated text in the adjacent column. An example of this is seen in Figure 1.

This greatly simplifies the task for there is always the danger of missing a word, a phrase or even a sentence if you decide to translate a text document directly from a printed or an electronic copy. On the occasions when this has to be done, it is very frustrating to keep two

Figure 1. A CAT software interface, with source language on the left, and target language on the right.

documents side by side and synchronised on a computer screen.[4] The source and target are always synchronised in this type of software and they stay that way as the translation progresses.

### 3.3.1 Q&A

The advantages don't stop there though. One of the key features is the so-called Q&A which means that the software analyses the translation that you have made and checks that things are consistent. For example, it can do a spellcheck, which of course a regular editing software can do. However, it can also check that you have copied the numbers or dates correctly. It is so easy to make a mistake here and wrong numbers are a sure indication of a sloppy or inexperienced translator and will inevitably mean that you will not get work from that agency or client again. It can also check that the punctuation is consistent with the source at least where it should be, and if there are extra spaces that have crept into your target text. This is particularly useful as it is difficult to find these spaces when looking at the target column. The machine will do this for you.

One of the things that you should do after performing a CAT translation, however, is to output the document (if you can) into Word (for example) and look at what the text looks like on the page. Here is a second chance to find spelling errors, spaces and inappropriate punctuation. Read it through. If you rely too heavily on machine analysis of your document, you should remember that a mistyped word may in fact be a real word and a spellchecker will not find this. We say again, read it through.

---

[4] Having two screens can be a help here.

Another feature that Q&A analysis can offer is checking for repeated words. This can happen very easily especially if you revise "on the fly", i.e., as you go along in the translation. "the the" is a favourite but there are lots of other cases.

### 3.3.2 Translation memories and consistency

In technical translations, there are many cases where whole sentences will be repeated exactly. This is particularly true when translating instruction manuals or maintenance manuals. This can also happen from one document to another and it is here that these CAT tools earn their money. (The major ones are not cheap (several hundred Euros) but getting into translation requires some expenditure. They quickly pay for themselves though).

When you type a sentence in the target column, corresponding to the source column, what you enter is immediately saved by the computer in a translation memory. You confirm this translation by a keystroke or two, and you go to the next line. The computer then searches through the translation memory to see if the next source line is at least approximately the same as what you have entered, and if so, it enters the target text automatically. (This is NOT machine translation — these are your words). In fact, things are more complicated than that as the software can go through the entire remaining source text to find a repeated phrase and enter it automatically. (This automatic feature can be turned on or off depending on the circumstances).

Furthermore, let's say you have translated a similar document before and there are sentences in it that are the same as in your current document. Well then, the software will find these phrases in the translation memory you created when working on the earlier document, and it will then search this to see if the source text you have to translate has already been translated in the earlier document. If so, it will enter it into your target automatically or upon request. This is really an extraordinary feature and if you think about it, you will be amazed as to how much this software is doing for you. They are very sophisticated programs.

Actually, when setting up your translation project, and having specified which of your translation memories you want to use, the software will prepare the work by searching the translation memory and will automatically fill already translated lines, even before you sit down to translate. Translation memories are the translator's gold because if you are lucky enough to get a recurring project with repeated phrases, they save you a lot of work and earn you money (by saving time).[5] When you think about it, this is an amazing functionality as it saves so much time as well as remembers how you translated that phrase the last time.

When you learn to write essays at school, you are encouraged to say the same things differently to make the text more interesting. This actually does not really apply to technical translation where the goal is to be accurate and understandable. If you call an object five different ways in a manual, you risk totally confusing the reader. Better to stick to what you called it the first time. It is in this spirit that the translation memory concept is applied.

At this point though, an awful spectre has to be raised and that is Murphy's law. In general terms, Murphy's law states that "Anything that can go wrong, will go wrong". In our experience, a form of Murphy's law can be applied to translating:

> "Any sentence in a translation that is repeated will probably have at least one error in it. And the more times the sentence is repeated, the more likely this is to occur".

Murphy was an xx?!XX but some say he was an optimist!

### 3.3.3 *Termbases and consistency*

This is another feature of CAT tools that is a great time saver and aids in consistency. You could say that a termbase (database of terms) is a glossary. Let us say that you are translating a text about a nuclear reactor and you find that the term *grappe* is used. If you look up a general

---

[5] Although it has to be said that often repetitions are not paid.

French dictionary, you will find that this is given as "cluster" in English. For instance, a cluster of grapes. But what has that to do with a nuclear reactor? (Machine translation would love this example!). The thing is that Technical Translation is all about context. When you are doing a translation, you would know what the context is — nuclear, construction, aeronautics, railway technology, electricity production and transmission, etc. Every domain has its own terminology (or jargon sometimes) and you have to understand where you are before taking on a translation. We shall talk about this in much more detail in later chapters.

OK, if you can find a good nuclear glossary, you will learn that *grappe* refers to a cluster or bundle of fuel rods or control rods (thus not so far from a vineyard as you might think!). A *doigt-de-gant* is not a glove finger but a well in which a thermocouple is fitted — a thermowell. It can also be called a "thimble" which is a tube structure. Things quickly get complicated and if you come back to this type of translation after not having worked on the subject for months or years, you might forget such points. And here is where the termbase comes in.

A termbase is a bit like a translation memory but it applies to words or word strings. When you find the right target term for a source word, you can enter it into your termbase manually and the next time you come across it further down the document or in another document altogether, the software will give you the translation for this source term when it crops up. This means that you have to load the particular termbase before starting the translation. You build your own glossaries for the subject matter you are working on.

Again, this makes up some of the translator's gold reserve.

Termbases are more than glossaries though, and can be a great help in any translation where a word is repeated many times. Let's say you are working on a document concerning the famous company Widget, Inc. They are very proud of their name and use it often throughout the text. Now you could type this in each time you come across it but it is simpler to add this name into the termbase, so that the next time it appears in the document, you just type "W" and the word will automatically appear in a drop-down list. (You may have added other words at different times and in different documents, such as Water, West, Wright-Patterson Airforce Base…so be careful that you choose the right offering in the drop-down menu otherwise things become confusing to say the least). The point is that this saves a lot of re-typing and thus time.

Having words in a termbase also helps in maintaining consistency in a translation. This is especially true if you are working on a large project along with other translators or if you will be working on the same subject matter over the long term. Building a common termbase is essential for making sure that everyone is using the same translated terms and this may be managed by the agency that has contracted with you to work on the project. It has to be said though that this may also introduce a complication for you. If you have been provided with a termbase from the client or the agency, and if you do not use their terminology or you forget to check the termbase, you will receive complaints that may require a rework of the translation.

So the bottom line is, get to love your termbase and pay lots of attention to it.

### 3.3.4 *Agencies, translation memories, termbases and packages*

This is another feature of CAT tools. When working with translation agencies, they often have their own preferred tool, be it Trados, MemoQ, etc. And sometimes instead of just sending you a text document, they will send you a package. So what is a package? Well it is a set of files that include the text to translate already converted into the form that the particular software can use, together with a translation memory and a termbase. You enter this into your software (that either you own personally, or some agencies will send you a one-time licence), you do the translation, and you produce a return package with updated translation memory (but not updated termbase which is usually locked). This has advantages and disadvantages. The first is that the project is ready to work (turn-key) and you don't have to worry about the form of the output. That is up to the agency. The disadvantage is that generally you cannot produce the output yourself so proofreading must be done within the CAT and you cannot check the output form yourself. It also means that sharing the project between two different computers is complicated because once you open a package in one computer, you cannot close it and transfer it to another computer. It will not work. It sometimes happens that the person who has produced the package has made an error somewhere and some features do not work. This is just one technical problem that can arise.

### 3.3.5 *Technical problems with CAT tools*

*Input*

Let's forget about packages now and suppose you are given a document to translate. Let us say it is a Word document. No problem. When you create your project in your CAT tool, you enter the file directly, the software processes it, prepares the source and target columns, the translation memory if any, fills in already translated segments, etc. You do the translation and you still have a half-hour to go before the delivery deadline.

*Output*

You then ask the software to output the file back as a translated Word document. If all goes well, you have a document with a formatting similar to what went in. BUT. Sometimes you get error messages that are incomprehensible. You cannot produce the output. Panic sets in. At this stage, head for the Internet, type in your error message and see what the community says. Sometimes this can be as simple as re-entering the source file with a different Word version and letting the translation memory re-translate it for you. This is a problem that arises sometimes with Trados Studio that despite many reincarnations still has quite a few bugs. Remember that these are very sophisticated programs so don't be too surprised when things go wrong.

One thing to do when you start a translation is that sooner rather than later, do a trial output to make sure that you can produce the output. If there is a problem, this will give you time to sort it out. Don't leave it to faith and the last minute.

As I say, if an agency sent you a package, this is their problem and generally they know how to fix it. If the text should happen to be your own, this will not cause you problems. Usually, the problem comes from what an agency has sent you and in what form.

*Input (again)*

What if you are sent a PDF or an Excel file or a Powerpoint? These days you can enter these directly into Trados Studio or MemoQ and it will take care of the formatting and the output will look like the input. In a perfect world. However, some PDFs are not accepted directly for some reason. Who knows why? In this case you can turn to a commercially available software that converts PDFs into Word format. This is called OCR or Optical Character Recognition Software. This was what you had to do in earlier versions of these CAT tools but nowadays this feature is directly incorporated. If it works. If not, use OCR software! Some PDFs are of such poor quality (scanned documents) that nothing will work and you might have to set aside the CAT tool to do the job.

*Output (again)*

When things work perfectly, this is a rather seamless process. Sometimes though, you run into formatting issues and some pesky parts refuse to go where they should. Some parts of a document may in fact be in the form of an image and this can be placed incorrectly in the output. This is a headache that can take time and bitten fingernails to fix.

Trados, in particular, does not like Excel files with multiple columns and gets totally messed up. MemoQ works better with these. Generally, MemoQ gives fewer problems but if the agency has invested thousands of Euros in the professional version of Trados Studio (which can be used to create packages for example), you will be forced to work with that.

*Conclusion*

As you can see from the above, CAT tools can be of great help to the translator when things go well…which they usually do. It is just wise to be aware that things don't always go well and be prepared to work around them.

## 3.4 Machine Translation

We mentioned machine translation in the first part of this book and basically the advice given holds for those doing Direct Translation. Don't use it. Do not use it. Google translation is OK for trying to understand a Bulgarian website or even a Korean patent, but it is not capable of giving the average user an acceptable, professional rendering of your text. In addition, it poses a real problem for the proofreader you have asked to clean up your text. Sometimes it is really difficult to understand what it has produced as the grammar, terminology and structure are all wrong.

But let's look at it from the translator's point of view. As a translator, again our advice is don't try to use it to produce your translation. Sometimes the work you hand in does not satisfy the client who says that the translation is too literal (word-for-word) and you get accused of using machine translation. To us, this is a serious insult for a professional translator should not stoop so low as to use it. OK, maybe you are not William Shakespeare or Molière but you have done your best to produce an accurate translation, even though it may not sound very literary. (We suspect sometimes this response is used to get the price dropped. Like any business, translation can be cutthroat).

Right then, we have agreed, we are not going to discuss how you can get the best out of machine translation for doing your translation. But this subject will simply not go away.

The translation business has changed quite dramatically in the last couple of years and now it is quite common to be offered jobs that involve what is called "post-editing". This is not "proofreading" where you read through a document and pick up the odd spelling mistake or wrong number and, occasionally and critically, the wrong terminology. This is where you are given a text that has already been machine translated and you have to produce a clean document from it. To put this in monetary terms, if you can charge an amount X per word for straight translation and 0.1–0.2X for proofreading, post-editing should be paid 0.5–0.6X per word (or even more).

Some translation agencies now use machine translation themselves to produce a first draft of a document and then contract with you to clean it up. Typically, this is when they have very established clients and delivery hundreds of thousands or millions of words in many, many different documents, but on a specific subject. For example, JBAM has worked for five or six years for a particular agency for a client that is a major equipment manufacturer. The work involves specifications for equipment and maintenance manuals. This work is very meticulous and involves the kind of detail you come across in Technical Translation. The fact is that this type of work is rather, or indeed, very repetitive and so very large translation memories have been established on this subject. It was natural, therefore, that this agency would turn to machine translation to streamline the process. This allows them to drop their prices and to compete in a very competitive industry. Of course, this price reduction gets passed on to the translator and so in principle your income drops. It is an unfortunate fact of life. The theory goes, however, that if you do it well, you will get more work and if truth be told, in this particular instance this is true.

As an aside, we can mention a different type of approach that we encountered with another agency where the manuals were partly written in English by the engineers themselves. This was a massive project but we were paid to translate the parts in French while the documents rendered contained the self-translated part. Unfortunately, the so-called "English" turned out to be rather "Franglais" and so we ultimately got blamed for not doing a good job and have not worked with that agency since. Such is life but it was a painful experience. The thing to take away from this is:

> "Beware of the client who does the job themselves and asks you to clean it up."

Back to machine translation. While at first we were very sceptical of this new approach, it turns out that the translations we were asked to post-edit were actually very good. The programs employed to do the job used artificial intelligence to find the context and the correct terminology, based on the massive database of previous translations. But you still have to be very careful and read every sentence, every word, very carefully to make sure that it is correct. It has to be said this is a very tedious process and much more intense than straight proofreading. This is a specific case however, and for subjects where artificial intelligence (or, as it is now known, "deep learning") cannot be effectively applied, the results can be awful. And then you have your work cut out for you (and at a reduced price) to fix up the mess.

Synonyms are a trap in machine translation. *Fission, scission, division, separation, split,* for instance, are used interchangeably even by a good algorithm. However, the right word depends on the context. In one translation that we did concerning surgical instruments, one term was used repeatedly in the source document. This was *trépan* which in English is:

"trephine".

The machine had real problems here and came up with a wide variety of translations for this term including:

"trephine, spot, pitch, trespan, stripe, laptops, streak, trunk, stop valve, pad, trephine-blade".

The term *lame-trépan* ("trephine blade") was translated as "laser-tray"!

A word of warning. Post-editing requires very special attention to be paid to errors that can occur that are easily overlooked. For example, take the sentence:

*Déposer les trois vis CHC M4 (8), les trois rondelles CS (9) et les trois rondelles plates (10) de fixation du ventilateur (5).*

Here the screws (*vis*) and washers (*rondelles*) are specified as to their type (CHC M4, CS and flat (*plates*), respectively), but are also identified on a drawing by their respective item numbers (8), (9) and (10). The machine translation for this phrase was:

> "Remove the three CHC M4 (8) screws, three CS (9) washers and three flat (10) fan retention washers (5)."

But this is wrong for now the identifiers (in brackets) have been mixed in with the characteristic of the screws and washers. What is especially serious is that a human translator would not have done this, so this is an immediate indication that this sentence has been machine translated. Hence the final client will understand that their document has been machine translated and of course, the translation should be a transparent process.

To reinforce this point, we should like to mention a message that we received very recently from a translation agency located in Vienna, Austria that pertains directly to this subject:

> Due to current events, we feel the need to clarify the workflow on Machine Translation (MT) vs. human translation. We have noticed on several occasions now that some colleagues use deepL or other MT engines for translating our projects, without having it brought to our attention first. We know the engines have become able to produce good translation quality; however, you MUST tell us if you're planning on using MT when working on our projects!
>
> We are certified according to ISO 17100 and ISO 18587, which means that we must deliver a human translation if that is what the client orders. If we deliver an MT without telling the client, this constitutes a breach of contract. We offer MT for highly repetitive and standardised texts or in cases the client needs a translation fast. For MT, the price per word is reduced.
>
> text-it Produktdokumentation GmbH, Vienna, 2021

So the bottom line here is, don't try this at home! Leave it to the experts to produce the first draft if that has been agreed with the client and don't try to take this shortcut when doing translations as it breaches your contract with your contracting agency.

However, we wish our book to be not only informative but also to have a few "light" moments when reading through it so, where appropriate, we shall include a few "precious" machine translations, to illustrate how things can go wrong.

## 3.5 Internet Searching

It is difficult to imagine how complicated technical translation must have been before the advent of the World Wide Web. Certainly, it would have entailed having shelf loads of expensive dictionaries unless you restricted yourself to a single or at most a few specific areas. Indeed, we do have shelf loads of dictionaries, though we use them less and less. Why? Because it is quicker to look things up on the Internet and also, we have some dictionaries in electronic form and this speeds up searching. Having said that, it is comforting to have an actual, physical document in your hands that you can flip through and maybe get context from. This is particularly true if your dictionary happens to come with illustrations, like the "Dicobat" dictionaries that we will discuss in Section 4.8 on Construction.

Terminology is the key issue in technical translation and it is essential to master the ability to find the right term. One of us gave presentations at a translator's conference some years ago on exactly this subject. It is not enough to simply go to a dictionary, find the word in the source text and plug in what the dictionary gives you. Throughout this book, we have given a number of examples of how a given word can mean different things to different people. Context is everything. You have to have the glossary in your mind for the subject you are translating. If you are lucky, your client will provide you with it, but don't hold your breath as they say. Our experience is that client-provided glossaries often contain all the words you don't need but not the ones you do. Maybe this is why you were hired in the first place? To complete their glossary. If you are provided with a glossary though, it is essential that you do use it. This is where having a termbase is such a useful thing when using CAT tools, for often the glossary can be incorporated directly into the tool. On occasions, the client will give you translations of terms that are not correct but as Alfred Lord Tennyson said in his poem *The Charge of the Light Brigade*, "Theirs not to reason why, Theirs but to do and die". It is the client that pays the bills and if they insist, you have to use their terms, or their style of writing.

Okay, but how can you use the Internet to find the right terms? There are several approaches to this. One is to use multilingual online dictionaries such as Termium, Reverso, Lingua (a particularly poor one, but which can put on the right track for a true search, especially for legal and administrative documents), Wordreference, etc. You type the word you are looking for, e.g., *palier* along with *traduction*, or *anglais*, and you will be directed to one of these sites that will give you a selection of choices for the translation. It has to be said that these sites are based on Internet searches for where these terms have been used so their correctness is somewhat subjective. You have to take things with a pinch of salt, as they say, i.e., healthy scepticism and ready criticism.

This particular example, *palier*, is interesting for it is one of the words in French that have numerous meanings, most often "bearing" in a mechanical engineering context, or "landing" on a stairway in a construction context, or "level" in administrative documents. Recently, we were translating a document on nuclear power, where the proofreader (a person experienced in technical translation) objected to the fact that we translated this word as "plant series" instead of "bearing". After all the document did talk about motor pumps in some parts, and one would think that "bearing" was the appropriate choice. However, this was a case where the client, the operator of nuclear power plants, has a very extensive and specific glossary and for them, *palier* refers to the fleet (*parc*) of power plants with nuclear reactors of various kinds (PWR, BWR, EPR, etc.). Hence, "plant series".

We would like to mention the organisation "ProZ", which is a clearing house for translation and where clients can go to find matching translators. We have been members of ProZ for many years and have benefitted greatly from it. One of the features on their website is called Kudoz, and this is where translators can ask for translations of terms they have come across and the question is thrown open to the ProZ public who choose to participate. If you have a good idea, you give an answer to this question, and if your suggestion is accepted on a majority vote, then you receive "Kudoz points". It is a good way to achieve notoriety in the field and may help you to get more work proposals. You can access this service as a look-up method by, for example, typing *palier proz* in your search engine and this will lead you to the ProZ website with the suggestion given for the proposed translation of the term. It is useful for the context of the term is usually given in the original request. We have found this particularly useful when searching for widely used administrative terms, but you must remember that the answer you find is based on the opinions of those who have made the suggestions. Again, a good pinch of salt is needed.

There are times, however, when your search through these dictionaries/glossaries does not produce a satisfactory result. What do you do then? Well, you start working the Internet. Internet searching is mysterious and Google has perhaps one of the best search engines. How it works is of course a closely guarded secret and, in the language of computer science, is not "transparent" to the user. However, we can make use of Boolean logic to track down the right term. In this case it is the AND function, although in the case of Google typing the AND command is not necessary. Thus, if you want to find the "in-context" translation or explanation for *palier*, you could type *palier EDF* (for *palier* AND *EDF*). The AND function means that the return to your request must contain *palier* AND *EDF*. This may not lead you to the translation itself but to a document where the specific context of the use of the term can be found. From there, you can formulate the right term in your target language.

Let's try some exercises here. Below there are a series of questions asking you to find the right term to use in a given context. Some of these you will have already seen in this book but have a go at finding these terms for yourself. The examples given are French words but this is a good exercise if you are approaching it from another source language where the target language is English.

1) **Lunette** in Mechanical Engineering
2) **Lunette** in Automobile engineering
3) **Lunette** in Astronomy
4) **Lunette** in Medicine
5) **Coupon** in Mechanical Engineering
6) **Coupon** in Commerce
7) **Soudure** in Electronics
8) **Soudure** in Nuclear Engineering
9) **Gamelle** in Automotive Engineering
10) **Assiette** in Aviation
11) **Action** in Finance
12) **Action** in Quality Control
13) **Résultat** in Finance
14) **Résultat** in Physics
15) **Réaliser** in Construction
16) **Réaliser** in Psychiatry

We shall not supply answers to these as we have done for the exercises in the individual sections in Chapter 4. Instead, we leave it up to the reader to explore these different threads.

# Chapter 4

# Specific Technical Fields

## 4.1 Abbreviations/Acronyms

If you live and work in France, you will find that you will be quickly submerged in acronyms. I (JBAM) remember receiving an e-mail from a colleague that contained 24 of them. I wrote back asking for what they meant and in fact my colleague did interpret them for me. Indeed, their e-mail would have been several pages long. People in this country seem to be comfortable with it and most of the governmental organisations are readily identified by them:

- *CNRS* — *Centre Nationale pour la Recherche Scientifique*
- *CEA* — *Commissariat à l'énergie atomique et aux énergies alternatives*
- *INSERM* — *Institut national de la santé et de la recherche médicale*
- *INRA* — *Institut national de la recherche agronomique*

etc. etc. University laboratories (actually these are what an English-speaking person would call "Departments") are almost always identified by their acronym:

- *IPR* — *Institut de Physique de Rennes UMR 6164 du CNRS* (The Physics Department)

- *IETR — Institut d'Electronique et des Technologies du Numérique (UMR 6164 du CNRS)* (The Electrical Engineering Department)
- *ISCR — Institut des Sciences Chimiques de Rennes (UMR 6226 du CNRS)* (The Chemistry Department)

UMR stands for *Unité Mixte de Recherche* which means that it is an organisation that has both University personnel and personnel who are members of the CNRS and this organisation receives support from the CNRS. Life gets complicated. Of course, there are many acronyms in English as well:

- NASA — National Aeronautics and Space Administration
- NSF — National Science Foundation
- DOE — Department of Energy
- USAF — United States Air Force

But there is not the proliferation seen in France. We shall discuss acronyms throughout this book as some fields (e.g., Aeronautics) are laden with them. For the moment, let us just talk about the use of acronyms in scientific publications.

### 4.1.1 Use of acronyms in scientific publications

There are many acronyms that have crept into the various fields of science over the years. For example, we are all familiar with:

DNA — Deoxyribonucleic acid,

although when we Googled it, we found:

*Dernières Nouvelles d'Alsace* (Latest News from Alsace).

Right there, you can see the danger of using acronyms, not that any self-respecting scientist would confuse this particular example. Modern chemical and physical analysis has invented quite a zoo of them:

- XPS — X-Ray Photoelectron Spectroscopy (That used to be called ESCA — Electron Spectroscopy for Chemical Analysis)
- EXAFS — Extended X-Ray Absorption Fine Structure
- NEXAFS — Near Edge X-ray Absorption Fine Structure
- XANES — X-ray Absorption Near Edge Structure
- SAXS — Small Angle X-Ray Scattering
- SANS — Small Angle Neutron Scattering

etc. etc. These are internationally recognised terms, and you can use them freely in scientific papers, though it is always a good idea to give the full title at least once so that the reader is not confused.

What you should avoid doing is inventing acronyms so that you can then use them throughout your article to save yourself typing, unless you can really justify their use. They might find their way into the general literature, but probably not unless you have invented a new method or technique. They would probably make the reading of your document less clear and possibly tedious. When you look at a scientific article because you want to, for example, find the ionisation potential of a particular molecule, you may skip the introductory paragraphs and if you are suddenly confronted with acronyms that seem to you important, you now have to scan through the document to find their meaning. Some journals (e.g., *Combustion and Flame*) ask authors to provide a list of acronyms at the beginning of their text and this can be helpful but if there are too many, it is onerous having to skip backwards and forward to check what PIV, FRS and PLIF mean.[1] If you are used to working in a given field, this may not seem a problem to you as you may use this language but remember, your paper might be read by someone who has only a cursory knowledge of your field and who is looking for something very specific.

One area where acronyms are perfectly fine to use is when you are referring to a group of authors, so (SJV) is "natural" to use if you refer several times to a paper by Smith, Jones and Velikovsky.[2] You will have

---

[1] Particle image velocimetry, filtered Rayleigh scattering, planar laser-induced fluorescence.
[2] Don't try this with high energy physics papers with 200 authors!

included their paper in your list of references and it is easy for the reader to check this as they read through the text. Another example is where authors who have produced a particular method that is named after them find themselves becoming acronyms, e.g., the BBGKY hierarchy stands for Bogoliubov–Born–Green–Kirkwood–Yvon.

We shall discuss this topic later on in this book as it is a real problem when doing technical translations where there is no English equivalent to the acronyms that are encountered.

> (JBM) I remember being asked during a conversation on literature if I liked GBS. I had to stare at the person until they explained that they were referring to George Bernard Shaw. I thought I had heard GBH and they were talking about "Grievous Bodily Harm" which is a legal offence in the UK.

### How should you treat acronyms?

Rule number 1: Ask the client. Ideally, they will tell you what their acronyms mean and how they want them transposed in the target document: as they are, explained, etc. (there is more than one possible answer). Rule number 2: Make sure you understand what the acronym stands for. Let us take a tricky example:

*PAC de XXX prenant en compte l'actualisation des volumes de confinement.*

PAC = *pompe à chaleur* (heat pump)? Easy to find, but will not do.

Well, you kind of guess the PAC is a file because it says somewhere else *PAC déposé le XXX* ("PAC filed on XXX").

OK, you will find *Politique Agricole Communale* ("Communal Agricultural Policy"). Hmm, it does not really fit.

"information dossier PAC prefecture" is about what you think you know about this PAC as you are dealing with an "AP" (*arrêt préféctoral*), still nothing.

But oh miracle, when you type in "information dossier PA préfet", you get a wonderful *Contenu du Porter à Connaissance (PAC) du Préfet*...which reveals indeed what a PAC is, and since you really need to understand before attempting a translation, you can find the information in Wikipédia: https://fr.wikipedia.org/wiki/Porter_%C3%A0_connaissance. In fact a good translation of this is "Notice to the Public".

## 4.2 Physics

Let's start with a word that give English speakers particular trouble:

*courbature.*

When discussing diffraction, an important parameter is the "radius of curvature" and some native English speakers would call this *rayon de courbature*. When JBAM started teaching physics in France, he was surprised that his students laughed at him when he said this. The problem is that *courbature* means "muscle ache"!

The correct term is *rayon de courbure*, which is actually hard for a native English speaker to pronounce.

Generally though, physics does not present too many problems as far as terminology is concerned. Many terms such as "Bremsstrahlung", "Eigenvector (Eigenvektor)", "Gedanken experiment" are kept in their German form. The use of the Greek alphabet is widespread. "Tokamak" is a Russian word. Some terms are quite different, however.

Table 3 lists just a few examples but they give you a feeling that you should not be tempted to make too literal a translation and note where what you would think were the same, e.g., "positron, superconductivity" are actually slightly different in French.

Table 3. French and English physics terms that are quite different.

| French | English |
| --- | --- |
| *quantité de movement* | momentum |
| *posit(r)on* | positron |
| *Archimede* | Archimedes |
| *désintégration radioactive* | radioactive decay |
| *flottabilité* | buoyancy |
| *rotationel* | curl (function) |
| *faisceau* | beam |
| *courant de Foucault* | eddy current |
| *supraconductivité* | superconductivity |

Table 4. Naming of physics laws and theorems in English and French.

| English | French |
|---|---|
| Snell's law | *Loi de Snell-Descartes* |
| Shallow Water equations | *Equations de Barré de Saint-Venant* |
| Boyle's law | *Loi de Boyle-Mariotte* or *Loi de Mariotte* |

A word that is rather oddly used in French in an electrical context is *Intensité* or *Intensité de courant*, which is just "current" in English.

One area where French differs very greatly from that of English is the naming of laws and theorems, as shown in Table 4.

### 4.2.1 Fundamental differences

In the first section of this book, when discussing Direct Authoring, JBAM mentioned that the units of pounds and kilograms are not in fact equivalent, since the former is a unit of force while the latter, the kilogramme, is a unit of mass. Normally this is ignored, and one uses a simple conversion factor, i.e., 1 pound = 0.456 kilogrammes.

There are other equivalences that are less obvious, however. One that I (JBAM) liked to explain to my students was why synchrotron radiation, which was one of the tools I used in my research, should not work in France, despite the fact that there are two state-of-the-art machines there, the European Synchrotron Radiation Facility (ESRF) in Grenoble and Synchrotron Soleil in Saclay, near Paris. Let me explain...

In a synchrotron radiation facility, electrons are accelerated to high energies (Giga-electron volts or GeV) and then injected into a so-called electron storage ring, where they go round and round in a circular orbit for long periods of times (hours in older machines, but essentially indefinitely in modern machines with top-up filling from the injection accelerator). In reality, the orbits are not exactly circular as the machine consists of bending magnets and straight sections as illustrated in Figure 2. Hence, the machine has a rather scalloped appearance. To give you an idea of the size of such a machine, the circumference of the ESRF is about 1 kilometre.

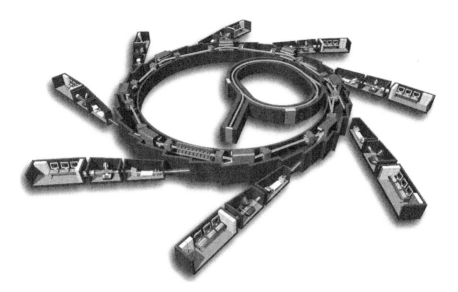

**Figure 2. Schematic diagram of Synchrotron Soleil. Copyright © EPSIM 3D/JF Santarelli, Synchrotron Soleil.**

The electron period, i.e., the time it takes for an electron to make one full orbit in the machine is kept constant. Thus the synchrotron used to produce synchrotron radiation is in fact not an accelerator but a storage ring. The initial acceleration of the electrons is produced by a linear accelerator and a booster synchrotron but this is really irrelevant to the synchrotron radiation user who is only interested in the radiation that comes out of the machine. Very uniquely intense, tunable radiation that can extend from infra-red radiation up to hard X-rays. For example, the X-radiation beam emitted by a so-called third-generation synchrotron is a billion times more intense that that emitted by a typical hospital X-ray machine, and while the latter emits at a single wavelength, synchrotron radiation appears as a wide continuous spectrum allowing, for example, X-ray spectroscopy to be performed on samples illuminated by the beam.

Our point here is not to discuss the field of synchrotron radiation research but to use it as an illustration to understand the difference between the terms "speed" and "velocity", something every science pupil in an English-speaking school will (or should) understand. As we just stated, the electron period in the storage ring is constant. If you like, the frequency (the number of times they rotate per second) is constant. Hence that means that their speed is constant. In French you would say the *vitesse* is constant. And this is where the problem comes in.

Maxwell's equations can be used to show that when an electrically charged particle, such as an electron, is accelerated, it will emit radiation. This is the fundamental phenomenon behind the emission of all electromagnetic radiation such as radio waves where electrical currents oscillate back and forth in an antenna (aerial). How is acceleration thus produced in a storage ring since the speed is constant? Well, an **acceleration** means that there is a change in **velocity** and we have bolded these terms since they are vectors, i.e., they are quantities that have both magnitude and direction. Thus the acceleration in a storage ring is achieved by changing the direction of the electrons and one of the ways of doing this is by "bending" the electron beam using a "bending magnet", and these are the devices that produce the electron orbits. (In fourth-generation machines, devices called "undulators" are used where the beam is made to wiggle as it moves along, under the influence of an array of alternating North and South pole magnet pairs. This enhances the output intensity by orders of magnitude). Every time the beam is "bent" it spews out radiation and since in a storage ring the electrons are relativistic (their speed is almost that of the speed of light), the radiation is forward directed in the form of a beam.

Thus the "velocity" (a vector) is changed by changing direction, while the "speed" (a scalar) is constant. But in French, "velocity" is *vitesse*, just like "speed", so in principle it should be constant, and a synchrotron storage ring should not work in that language!

Fortunately, France is a country that is renowned for its excellence in mathematics and so a purist will talk about the *vecteur vitesse*, so the machines do work, but in fact our experience indicates that most students do not know the difference between speed and velocity.

Another bit of French/English confusion concerns the mathematical entity "logarithm". As many a British schoolboy or schoolgirl can tell you, "logarithms" were invented by John Napier (1550–1617), a Scotsman. Hence, we can talk about Napierian logarithms. In French one speaks of *logarithme Népérien* which in English is known as the Natural Logarithm[3] (the inverse of the exponential function). So the French would say that it was Monsieur Néper who invented the logarithm. A classic bit of English/French "friendly" competition.

Some years later AIFM checked this story out and in fact they were one and the same person. **Napier** was the "anglicised" version of his Latin name **Ioannes Neper**, and the French chose **Jean Neper** to refer to him. However, as explained in https://fr.wikipedia.org/wiki/John_Napier, he was referred to by the following names as well: Napeir, Nepair, Nepeir, Neper, Nepper, Naper, Napare, Naipper, including several by himself!

When I (JBAM) set out to prepare my lectures in French, I was surprised to find that the term *self de choc* refers to an inductor, i.e., an electrical device introduced into a circuit to provide the property of inductance, much as a resistor provides resistance or a capacitor capacitance. These devices make up the RLC circuits that are used in radio transmission and reception apparatus. The term *self* I could understand as the inductor experiences what is called "self-inductance". This is a phenomenon studied by Michael Faraday where a coil of wire has the effect of opposing the movement of an electrical current that is changing with time such as an "alternating current" (and not "alternative current" which you might think since the French is *courant alternatif*). This is a type of knee-jerk or instinctive reaction of this device. What occurs is that the device "chokes" the flow of current and so it is often referred to as a "choke". I have the feeling that this is why the term *choc* is used in French which otherwise does not really make sense since in English, "shock" means "impact".

Density is an odd situation for what is called "density" in English is called *masse volumique* in French (i.e., mass per unit volume). What

---

[3] In fact Napierian logarithms are not the same as natural logarithms (see https://en.wikipedia.org/wiki/Napierian_logarithm) but we shall not go into the details here.

is called *densité* in French is called "specific gravity" in English. This is the "density" normalised to that of water ($\rho = 1000$ kg/m$^3$). (The specific gravity of water is thus 1 and that of mercury, for example, is 13.6). Note it is a quantity without units.

### 4.2.2 Exercises

Find the correct translation for:

1. *Moment cinétique*
2. *Coefficient directeur*
3. *Tracé*
4. *Couple*
5. *Grandeur*

## 4.3 Chemistry

There are many requests for chemistry translations involving Material Safety Data Sheets, tests and controls of pharmaceutical products and raw materials, etc. In fact, the field is vast so they can come from a very wide range of applications. There is even the occasional request for improving the English in a paper submitted for publication. Fortunately, this is a field where chemical names are standard, and it is a question of finding the English equivalent. Let's start with the elements (Figure 3).

Some names are the same in English and French, while others differ. Here are a few:

- N = *Azote* → Nitrogen
- Ag = *Argent* → Silver
- S = *Soufre* → Sulfur (Sulphur in UK English, non-standard)
- Fe = *Fer* → Iron
- Cu = *Cuivre* → Copper
- Au = *Or* → Gold
- Hg = *Mercure* → Mercury
- Sn = *Etain* → Tin

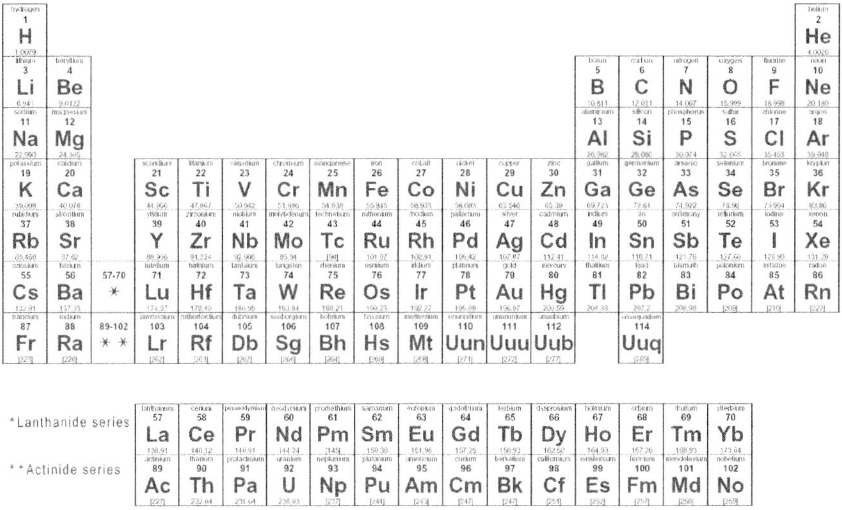

Figure 3. Periodic table of the elements. Copyright © LeVanHan, licensed under CC BY-SA 3.0.

- Cs = *Césium* → Caesium (Cesium in US English, non-standard)
- Pb = *Plomb* → Lead

Often French terms carry an *è* where in English there is a simple "e", for example:

$$\textit{Ethylène} \rightarrow \text{Ethylene}$$

while *-ique* in French becomes "-ic" in English:

$$\textit{Acide hydrochlorique} \rightarrow \text{Hydrochloric acid.}$$

Fortunately, most chemical names can be found on the Internet, but it is always best to check. In fact this is an area where, if you are in doubt, you should always check to make sure you have the correct translation of chemical names. There is a vast amount of knowledge on the internet for this.

If this is an area where you feel that you want to invest in, then it may be worthwhile to equip yourself with some basic reference works. This could be a university-level textbook in general chemistry, though if you are willing to take on translations in this area, you probably already have a decent background in it so these may already be in your arsenal. There are, however, a few that you might not have. In particular:

- Hawley's Condensed Chemical Dictionary 16th edition, Michael D. Larrañaga, Richard J. Lewis Sr. & Robert A. Lewis, John Wiley & Sons, Inc., New York (2016)
- Principles of Chemical Nomenclature: A Guide to IUPAC Recommendations 2011 Edition, G.J. Leigh (Ed.), RSC Publishing, London (2011).

Occasionally, you may come across a term that surprises you. For example, the word *sorbonne*. Almost everybody has heard of the prestigious and ancient French university *La Sorbonne*, named after Robert de Sorbon (1201–1274), chaplain to King Louis XI. In a humble chemistry lab however, the *sorbonne* is just what in English is called a "fume cupboard" or "fumehood"! A *bain-marie* has the more common name of "water bath" in English. As always, it is fascinating to look up things like this in Wikipedia to determine the origins of the word.

In fact, Wikipedia is a treasure trove of information on chemistry and a must-visit site when doing any translation on this subject. It is always wise to check any term you use for it is very easy to make mistakes because you think you know the right way to say it.

In the pharmaceutical industry, things become a lot more complicated because not only is there standard chemical terminology as you might expect, but you also run into trade names for pharmaceutical products and this can become confusing. Again, the Internet is a rich source of knowledge. If you expect to do a lot of pharmaceutical-type translations, investment in the Merck Index is well worth the cost.

We have mentioned the word "control" earlier in Section 1.2.10, which often means checking or monitoring, but in pharmacological production and testing, products undergo a "control procedure", that is they are checked for their purity and their conformance with the specifications. In this sense it is both a check and the "quality" is controlled, i.e., maintained constant.

As in any of these subjects, fundamental understanding and knowledge of the field is important and will allow you to avoid errors. For example, a term that is used a lot in French is *dosage*. Especially during pharmaceutical "controls". In English you can think of dosing yourself up with cough medicine if you are suffering from a cold (*rhume*). Hot whisky also works well for those that partake of it. You might be tempted to think that in this context, it refers to what you put into a product. What you dose it with. But then, when you think of medicine, you might think of what "dose" of antibiotic should you be taking. And here you get closer to what is meant.

When you are testing a product to establish its conformance with specifications, you need to know the concentration of the active ingredient in, for example, a pill or tablet (*un comprimé*) and this process is called *dosage*. Thus, the translation of *dosage* is, for example, "content" or "concentration determination". In fact, this term applies to what is called "volumetric analysis" in chemistry, where the concentration of a substance such as an acid in a solution is determined by titration. A sufficient, known quantity of alkali is added to the solution until it becomes neutral which is demonstrated by the colour change of an indicator such as litmus or phenolphthalein.

### 4.3.1 *Exercises*

Find the correct translation of:

1. *Gaz rare*
2. *Paillasse*
3. What does REACH refer to?
4. *Témoin*
5. *Solution-mère*
6. *Squelette carboné*
7. *Taux de réaction*

## 4.4 Aeronautics

This type of work involves specifications for aircraft, maintenance manuals, maintenance reports, descriptions of air traffic control systems, and anything involving aviation in general. The two major companies are of course Airbus and Boeing but there are lots of smaller outfits that need their documents translated.

Our recommendation for this type of work is to love flying, to love aircraft, to go to aircraft museums like the US Air Force Museum in Dayton, Ohio, the National Air and Space Museum in Washington DC, the Musée de l'Air et l'Espace in Le Bourget, Paris, or as was a memorable experience, the Romania Air Museum in Bucharest. For those who don't know, the French and the Romanians were some of the major pioneers in Aviation and Henri Coanda, who was a Romanian educated in France, set out the theory of flight (the Coanda Effect) as well as designed the first jet engine. Hermann Oberth, also Romanian, wrote the book on Rocketry and was the inspiration for Werner von Braun, who built the Saturn V rocket that took the astronauts to the moon. I (JBAM) can still remember my amazement when in Dayton, I saw the Wind Tunnel the Wright brothers built to test their models before trying the real thing, or as a child, sheltering with my father underneath the wing of a giant V-bomber during a rain shower at an air show in Northern Ireland. To have visited Cape Canaveral and heard the roar of the Saturn V rocket engines during a simulated launch. In other words, it helps to know your stuff.

But this type of translation is unforgiving. English is the lingua franca of aviation.[4] Every international commercial pilot must be able to speak English in order to talk to Air Traffic Control (ATC). What does this mean? It means that the pilot is expecting to hear the words that they know. The pilot is listening over a radio link that may or may not be of good quality. Their accent may be difficult for ATC to

---

[4] This is not quite true. The dreaded warning "Mayday, Mayday" is actually *M'aider, M'aider* (short for *venez m'aider*; Help me, help me) and "Pan-Pan" is *Panne, Panne* (Breakdown, breakdown).

**Figure 4. Aeronautical dictionaries by Thierry Goursau.**

understand. As a translator then, you have to know these words and don't try to make up ones that you think might be appropriate or sound right. This means that when you are working on an aeronautical translation, you do it with your Aeronautical Dictionary in your hand and you check EVERYTHING. The lives of many people might depend on it. Figure 4 shows what we use. Two well-thumbed books prepared by Thierry Goursau who has produced some really great French-English-French dictionaries that you can trust and depend on. If French is not your source language, you must search for this type of resource.

First of all, let's look at the parts of an aeroplane. Figure 5 shows one example of a typical commercial aircraft. You should get to know these parts, and all the better if you know how an aircraft flies. Let's look at who operates the aircraft. The "flight crew" includes the:

- Captain (PIC — Pilot in Command)
- First Officer (FO) or Co-pilot
- Cabin Crew

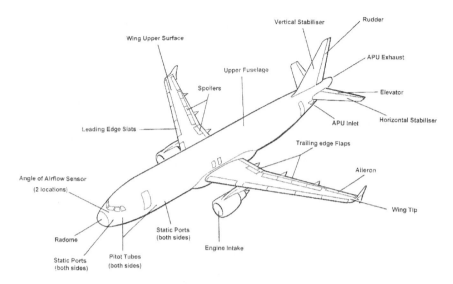

**Figure 5.   Parts of an Airbus A320. Public domain.**

- Pilot Flying (PF)
- Pilot Not Flying (PNF)

You should note that though the Captain (in the left-hand seat in the cockpit) is ALWAYS in command, he or she may not be the person flying the plane at any given moment such as during take-off or landing. This is because First Officers (in the right-hand seat) need to get experience in these manoeuvres and are often given this responsibility. Of course, you also have the Ground Crew and the Maintenance Crew.

One of the things you will notice is there are lots of abbreviations used. This is one area in English that is in fact swamped by abbreviations. (Normally many less abbreviations are used in English than in French for example, which makes translating these complicated). Fortunately, in aeronautics everything is standardised and it is possible to find long lists of these on the Internet at sites such as:

- http://www.airfleetuk.com/downloads/Aviation_Acronyms.pdf
- https://www.casa.gov.au/about-us/site-information/aviation-abbreviations-and-acronyms
- https://www.faa.gov/jobs/abbreviations/

- https://www.aviationtoday.com/2010/12/01/aerospace-acronym-abbreviation-guide/

to name a few. Speeds are very important for flying and Figure 6 is a list of these along with their acronyms.

Weights are also important (http://adg.stanford.edu/aa241/structures/totalweights.html):

- Maximum Taxi Weight (MTW): The certified maximum allowable weight of the airplane when it is on the ground.
- Maximum Brake Release Weight (MBRW): The certified maximum weight of the airplane at the start of take-off roll.
- Maximum Landing Weight (MLW): The certified maximum weight of the airplane at touch-down.
- Maximum Zero Fuel Weight (MZFW): The maximum weight of the airplane without usable fuel.

| Abbreviation | Term |
| --- | --- |
| $V_a$ | maneuvering speed |
| $V_{fe}$ | maximum flaps extended speed |
| $V_{le}$ | maximum landing gear extension sp |
| $V_{lo}$ | maximum landing gear operating speed |
| $V_{mc}$ | minimum control speed |
| $V_{mo}$ | maximum operating speed |
| $V_{ne}$ | never-exceed speed |
| $V_{no}$ | normal operating speed limit |
| $V_s$ | stall speed |
| $V_{so}$ | stall speed in landing configuration |
| $V_x$ | best angle of climb speed |
| $V_y$ | best rate of climb speed |

Figure 6. Abbreviations for speed terms in aeronautics. From: http://www.flightsimaviation.com/rule-of-thumb/27_VSpeeds_Abbreviations_List.html.

- Operational Empty Weight (OEW): Manufacturer's empty weight plus standard and operational items.
- Manufacturer's Empty Weight (MEW): Weight of the structure, powerplant, furnishings, systems.

And then on the runway (http://en.wikipedia.org/wiki/Runway):

- Take-off Run Available (TORA): The length of runway declared available and suitable for the ground run of an airplane taking off.
- Take-off Distance Available (TODA): The length of the take-off run available plus the length of the clearway, if clearway is provided.
- Accelerate-Stop Distance Available (ASDA): The length of the take-off run available plus the length of the stopway, if stopway is provided.
- Landing Distance Available (LDA): The length of runway that is declared available and suitable for the ground run of an airplane landing.
- Emergency Distance Available (EDA): LDA (or TORA) plus a stopway.

As you see, all this becomes very complicated and it helps to know your way around this before setting out on such a job.

One of the things that turned up in a translation we had on an Air Traffic Control ADS-B (Automatic Dependent Surveillance-Broadcast) system was the word *piste*. In a general dictionary, you will probably get a translation about skiing, but as a seasoned aeronautical translator, you will of course translate this as "runway". BUT, in this context, the word *piste* actually referred to aircraft flight paths. So once again, to get the right term, you have to understand the context you are working in and if the word does not seem right, perhaps it is not. Hence, some advice when doing aeronautical translations:

- Never assume you know how to translate a term.
- Always check the term. Use the dictionary or do a targeted Internet search.
- Prepare to be surprised!

As a final word, if you want to keep yourself up to date with what is happening in Aerospace, we really recommend the weekly journal *Aviation Week and Space Technology*. A great read for the enthusiast and the professional!

### 4.4.1 Exercises

Find the correct translation for:

1. *Empennage*
2. *Turbopropulseur*
3. *Train avant (TAV)*
4. *Sauterelle*

## 4.5 Automotive Engineering

This is an active subject with again its own vocabulary. Unfortunately, here, the vocabulary is not necessarily standard and can vary from one company to another. However, at least from French-to-English, there is a good dictionary available that is a wealth of information (Figure 7). Again, it is from Goursau.

For other languages you should investigate the availability of such a reference. For example, in German, there is the Wyhlidal Dictionary of Automotive Engineering available at https://en.pons.com/translate/wyhlidal-automotive-engineering-german-english.

As in aeronautical translation, it is important to understand the components of vehicles and engines. We were going to put a very good diagram of an automobile engine here but for technical reasons we decided to let you search for it on the Internet. Look for "automobile engine" or "gasoline engine".

**Figure 7. Goursau Dictionary of Automotive Technology. (We also have the electronic version in both French-English and English-French).**

The petrol (gasoline) or diesel engine falls under the category of Internal Combustion Engine, known in French as a *Moteur Thermique*. As we move into the third decade of the 21$^{st}$ century and beyond, these are likely to be overtaken more and more by hybrid cars (having an internal combustion engine and an electric motor) and eventually electric cars with just the electric motor. Hence pistons, combustion chambers, exhausts and sparkplugs will give way to coils and magnets. However, much of the rest of the vehicle will remain the same with bodywork, doors, windows, wheels, axles, fairings, trim, etc. When doing an automotive translation, it is important to have a reasonable idea of what exactly you are describing though with the advent of computer-controlled systems, this becomes less and less easy.

Table 5. Differences between UK and US terminology in automotive engineering.

| UK | US |
|---|---|
| Bonnet | Hood |
| Petrol | Gasoline (or just "Gas") |
| Boot | Trunk |
| Dip Switch | Dimmer Switch |
| Bumper | Fender |
| Silencer | Muffler |
| Spanner | Wrench |
| Lorry | Truck |
| Car | Automobile |

One of the things to watch out for is the difference between US and UK terminology. Examples of these are given in Table 5.

When doing a translation of this type, it is important to check with the client or your agency which version of English you have to translate into. We had a problem once with an agency who announced in the middle of a big job that they had forgotten to tell us that the target was US English. This meant searching for "z" words instead of "s" words (e.g., "optimize" ↔ "optimise") and in the end we got blamed because we had not found them all. Better to establish this right from the start.

As with many fields in engineering, a given word can mean different things to different people. For example, the French word *lunettes* means spectacles for an optician but in the automotive industry, *lunette* is the rear back window of a car. We shall see another use for this term in Section 4.7 on Mechanical Engineering. Again, one of the fun aspects of Technical Translation is to try to figure out exactly what a given term means and this involves going to the Internet and hunting for it, given the context. Sometimes you will find the answer in Wikipedia, a wonderful resource as the subjects are often given in many different languages. This may involve a lot of cross-checking between different pages to see where the term appears and to compare the two versions in the different languages. In the case of car parts, you may be fortunate enough to come across a multilingual website of a parts supplier. Hopefully, the person who has translated their site has indeed gotten the terms correct through actual inside knowledge or research rather than using a dictionary or, worse, Google translate!

A term that is used a lot when discussing electrical systems in cars is *faisceau*. Someone with a scientific background might be confused by this as one immediately thinks of "beam", like a "beam of light". In this context however, it means a "wiring harness", i.e., a bundle of wires that divide out to connect the various electrical components in the car. If you are really not sure of a term, the best thing to do is to ask the client. In this field, they often have a good knowledge of how to translate a given word and sometimes the answer you get can be surprising. For example, we were doing a translation for a major French car manufacturer and we asked a question about a type of indicator lamp on the dashboard of the vehicle. The answer came back — it is called a "telltale"!

At this point, it is worth giving a word of caution. Often if you search for a word on the Internet, you may indeed find it, but on a foreign site. Unfortunately, there is no guarantee that they are actually using the correct term. What to do in this case is to take the English word and search for it to see if it is actually used (on UK or US English websites). If not, the chances are that it is an incorrect translation.

Another word of caution is to watch out for documents where some of the text has already been translated by in-house staff. This was the case in a very large, very technical project we worked on. In an assignment of 25,000 words, the actual document turned out to be 50,000 words, with half already translated. Unfortunately, the pre-translated parts turned out to be in very poor English but we were not mandated to deal with these nor did we have the time given the deadline. However, we ended up being criticised for the overall quality of the work.

One of the surprising things that a new resident of France will find is the concept of CV. Automobiles are classified according to their CV which are not their résumés, but their:

*chevaux fiscaux*

or "fiscal horses". Understand? No?

Well, if we tell you that our little Peugeot 108 had a CV of 4, the average for French cars is 6, a Ferrari GTC Lusso has a CV of 40 while that of a Bugatti Chiron is 213, I guess you can tell that you will pay a lot more when registering a Bugatti Chron than a Peugeot 108. If you have a registered French car, you can tell what CV it has by looking at your:

*Carte Grise* (column P6)

or "Registration certificate". Otherwise, you can calculate it if you know the amount of $CO_2$ your automobile emits and its maximum power in kilowatts. Confused? Don't worry, Wikipedia will explain things better (https://fr.wikipedia.org/wiki/Cheval_fiscal).

To make things more complicated, the amount you will pay for your *carte grise* depends on what region of France you live in. In other words, this is all about money.

But how powerful is your automobile? This book is written for scientists and people with technical "skills" (*compétences*) so this is a much more interesting question. For this you should check out how many:

*Chevaux-vapeur* (not CV)

your automobile[5] has. We can see a look of fear in your eyes, but relax. This is "Horse Power" (HP), defined by the power developed by a horse when raising a weight of 75 kg by 1 metre in 1 second, i.e., 1 HP = 735.5 watts.

## 4.5.1 *Exercises*

Find the correct translation for:

---

[5] You may have been asking why we always talked about an "automobile" instead of a car because of course in French, a *car* is a "coach".

1. *Fusée de l'essieu*
2. *Volant moteur*
3. *Durite*

## 4.6 Railways and Trams

This is a very specialised technological area where there is little available information in the form of compiled glossaries or dictionaries. Fortunately, there is a lot of information that can be gathered from the Internet concerning the operation of the railways, the "rolling stock" (the trains and the carriages, wagons, etc.) as well as the infrastructure itself.

Basically, a modern train or a tram (very similar in fact) consists of a means of propulsion (a locomotive or power car for a train and a motor car for a tram) as well as carriages (or cars) on a train and cars on a tram. Together these form a trainset that can travel as a single unit (SU) or two trainsets can be joined together to form a multiple unit (MU). Some trains are self-propelled and such a unit is called a "railcar".

A tram (Figure 8) is made up of different types of car. There is one Motor Car (MC) with a cab at each end of the trainset (sometimes referred to as a tramset) so that the vehicle does not have to turn around at the end of the line. In between, there are Intermediate Cars (IC) and Motorised Intermediate Cars (MIC) separated by Suspended Cars (SC). Trams run by means of electric motors and the power for them usually comes from overhead lines along which a catenary (attached to the tram) slides, transferring electrical current to the vehicle. The MCs and MICs are equipped with catenaries. In the centres of cities, overhead lines can be problematic, especially in narrow streets, and some cities (like Bordeaux for example) are equipped with a system whereby current is fed to the tram from an electrified track, much like what is used in an underground (metro) train. This is a much more complicated system since it is only electrified as the vehicle passes. It goes by the name of "Aesthetic Power Supply" (APS) as opposed to the Overhead Catenary Supply (OCS).

**Figure 8.  Modern tram powered by overhead catenary system. Copyright © Chabe01, licensed under CC BY-SA 4.0.**

The cars themselves roll on the tracks by means of bogies, usually flanged metallic wheels. The pair of wheels on each side of the track are called a "wheelset" and they are connected to bogies that can be either motor bogies (i.e., driven by an electric motor; see Figure 9) or trailer bogies (i.e., not motorised, just pulled along). These bogies are equipped with self-lubricating systems but also with sandboxes. This can be quite surprising to learn, but metal wheels running on a metal track do not always have the best frictional characteristics so for braking, starting, etc., the sandboxes spray sand onto the rails to improve the traction/braking characteristics.

The wheels themselves undergo wear in operation and so they have to be serviced in a specialised workshop, by means of a pit lathe that resurfaces the wheels. After this, the wheels have a different diameter and so the odometry system for determining the speed of the vehicle (and distance travelled) has to be recalibrated.

**Figure 9.** Motor bogie. Copyright © DAJF, licensed under CC BY-SA 3.0.

Trams (and trains) do not have steering wheels. The vehicle follows the tracks. Instead, they have a "controller" that governs the traction/braking operation of the vehicle. Manipulating the controller allows the driver to speed up or slow down. There is also a driving switch that determines the mode of running (normal, neutral and shunting).

The controller is usually fitted with a "dead man's switch", also known by the more assuring name of "Driver's Safety System". This is a push-button that the driver must repeatedly keep pressing while the vehicle is in motion. (In some systems, it is a pedal[6] rather than a push-button). If the push-button is pressed for too long, or not pressed on time, the emergency brakes of the vehicle are applied. This means that if the driver becomes incapacitated or inattentive for some reason, the vehicle automatically switches to safety mode, and will come to a stop.

Trams are very complex vehicles with very sophisticated Instrumentation and Control (I&C) systems that govern the electrical supply, the operation of the tram (especially the operation of the

---

[6] Called *pédale de l'homme mort* at the time, while today's systems pertain to *veille automatique* (see Wikipedia articles in English and French for interesting historic details).

door opening, closing and locking) and also the self-diagnosis of these systems. Thus, there are different types of computerised networks that provide information both for operation but also for troubleshooting using specialised computer programs (like TrainTracer). Much of the language involved in maintenance manuals for these systems is computer jargon and one has to be very careful as the instructions are often very repetitive and it is easy to confuse one instruction with another. (This is not only restricted to the translator but even to the authors of some of the maintenance manuals). It pays to be very awake to make sure that what is written is consistent with the steps of the maintenance programme.

Although trams (and trains) are built by major engineering companies such as Alstom, Bombardier or Siemens, these companies call upon supplier companies for parts and components and this gives rise to Calls for Tender documents, where very specific requirements are given as to the dimension, the materials, quality of parts such as seats or fittings, etc. Other documents are complete manuals, listing the individual parts of, for example, a car or a carriage. The individual parts are referenced as they appear on assembly drawings, down to the nuts and bolts holding the parts together. (One document we translated concerned the entryway for a TGV train and was 69 pages long!). The important thing in such translations is to keep very close to the original document, using the correct terminology and paying close attention to the *nomenclature* (the parts list is also known as a "Bill of Quantities").

When working with these major engineering companies, you will find that they have their specific language and you must follow this. For example, one company we have worked with insists that the word "failure" must be used instead of "fault".

Trains are similar to trams from a translation point of view. In France the high-speed TGV system (*Train à Grande Vitesse*) are also very compact systems operating as trainsets, running on bogies (Figure 10). Generally, the vehicles are referred to as Rolling Stock and trains "roll" along the rails. When talking about rails, in French you often see the phrase:

*voie en alignement et palier.*

Figure 10. French high-speed train (TGV) showing a single unit trainset with the catenary extended (raised). Copyright © André Marques, licensed under CC BY 2.0.

This means a:

> "straight and level track".

The rails are held separate and parallel by being fixed to "sleepers" (*traverses*).

When a train enters a station, a tunnel, or a bend, it is very important that it fits into the restricted area and that its outer parts do not collide with obstacles such as platforms or track equipment. There is a word that describes this in French:

> *gabarit.*

In English this is called:

> "structure gauge".

This is not to be confused with the term "gauge" as used to define the separation of the rails and that can change from one country to another.

On a TGV, the train manager (or conductor in English, not to be confused with the *Conducteur* in French who is the person that drives the train) often makes an announcement, where they ask passengers to use their mobile phones on the *plateforme*, rather than in the carriage itself. This is to avoid disturbing other passengers. By this, they do not mean that the person has to alight from (get off) the train in a station (*gare*) to make their call from the platform (*quai*). The *plateforme* they are referring to is actually the "entryway" onto the train, which in a TGV is separated from the carriage areas by sliding doors. A nice example of a *faux-ami*. Somehow, the correct term has not made its way into SNCF's[7] vocabulary although the term "vestibule" is beginning to be seen in some new technical documents. Similarly, the "passenger compartments" in trains and trams are referred to as *salles* but the term "saloon" can be used for trains.

We mentioned above how the "Driver's Safety System" can cause a train to stop on the tracks due to the application of the emergency braking (EB) system. Under normal circumstances, the train can be slowed down by the driver using the service braking (SB) system. Emergency braking is a very serious action if the train is brought to a standstill on the track for there may (and probably will) be trains following them that must be warned of this event. Thus railways, which we tend to take for granted, are equipped with incredibly complex signalling systems and train controllers, who operate from "signal boxes" (*postes de contrôle*), are trained on simulators much like pilots, where the instructor can introduce a wide variety of events and conditions. Information from "trackside", i.e., the signal box, is passed to the train either automatically by trackside signals, or by communications to the driver from the control centre. Along the track, there are various signals that act like traffic lights on a road but which are activated by the operator in the signal box or automatically by the software controlling the signals.

In Europe, the tracks are equipped with automatic signalling systems that use *balises* to communicate with the train. This can inform

---

[7] SNCF: *Société nationale des chemins de fer* (The French railway company).

the train that it is entering a restricted speed zone, or a tunnel for example. Note that the term is *balise* (or *Eurobalise*) and not "beacon" as a translator might think. This is an example where there is a language in use established by international conventions.

---

**Machine Translation Error 1**

If the traction is withdrawn from the drive system of the train, it will then roll in "freewheeling mode". In a translation that dealt with the testing of a train, there was the sentence:

*Les essais de marche sur l'erre*

which was translated as:

"The tests of walking on the earth"

instead of:

"Freewheeling tests"

*l'erre* being "freewheeling".

---

**Machine Translation Error 2**

The French preposition *à* can produce many wrong translations because of the dual meaning "at" / "to". Thus a sentence:

*Freinages à 60% de la Vitesse maximum seront réalisés*

was translated as

"Braking **at** 60% of the maximum speed shall be carried out"

which at first sight might seem to be the correct translation. However, this involved taking a train to its maximum speed before applying braking to an intermediate speed, so the actual translation should have been:

"Braking **to** 60% of the maximum speed shall be carried out".

This is an example of how difficult post-editing can be. It requires great concentration and each sentence must be treated in the context of the surrounding text. The French sentence also contains the verb "realised" that is translated in this case as "carried out". See earlier discussion in Section 1.2.10.

### 4.6.1 *Exercises*

Find the correct translations for:

1. *Canton*
2. *Carré*
3. *Clé Berne*

## 4.7 Mechanical Engineering

This is a fascinating field for translations and fortunately one where there is a great deal of resource material. We have a very well-used dictionary, again from Thierry Goursau, that is a mine of information and as you can see from Figure 11, it has seen a lot of use.

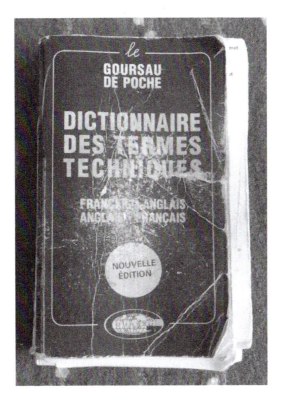

Figure 11.   The Goursau technical dictionary.

However, you have to understand what you are translating so that you can come up with the right term. It is no use guessing. For example, a word that gives a lot of problems is "bearing". This is a ubiquitous element of any system that involves movement as it is a device that allows the friction between moving parts to be eliminated by converting the mutual translational or rotational movement between two parts into the rotational movement of balls or rollers (needles) and then back to the two parts. Thus, for example, a wheel is fitted to an axle or shaft using a bearing so that it does not seize up when turning on the shaft as it would do from friction with the accompanying generation of heat and hence the expansion of the materials. Bearings come in many shapes and sizes and the rotating parts may be "ball-bearings" or "rollers". If the bearing is very small, these are referred to as "needles". To understand the importance of bearings, a lot of the Allied bombing effort during the Second World War was concentrated on factories that made ball-bearings. If you could not make these, tanks could not roll.

If you look up "bearing" in the trusty Goursau dictionary, you will find the following: *palier, bague, coussinet, roulement, porteur, surface d'appui, appui, portée de roulement, alésage, moyeu, gisement, azimut, relèvement (navigation)*. Some of these are mechanical bearings (or bearing holders): "*palier, bagues, coussinet, roulement*", while others refer to the use of the term when describing the support for something: "*appui, surface d'appui*", and some refer to navigation: "*azimut, relèvement*". It can be pretty embarrassing if you use completely the wrong term, hence the importance of having at least some background knowledge of the field you are setting out to translate in.

Another term that is confusing and that we encounter throughout this book is *contrôle*. Again, looking in the Goursau dictionary, you find: control, check, test, verification, inspection, monitoring, examination, supervision, audit, revision. You see here that this word means "checking" or "monitoring" rather than "controlling" something to make it do what you want it to. In fact, the French would rather use the term *commander* for this and sometimes you see the term *contrôle-commande*. You will see that indeed this term *contrôle* can be quite confusing and you really have to figure out what the author of the text is trying to say.

### 4.7.1 *Mechanical structures*

Mechanical engineering is all about making objects, whether an automobile, a bridge, a reactor vessel or anything else you can imagine that has a structure. The object can involve moving parts as in an engine, a train, an automobile, or it may be static as in a bridge, a pylon or a tank for holding liquids or gases. There are various methods for producing these objects whether as one-piece units or as assemblies of components. In the following we shall stick to parts that are essentially metallic.

For one-piece parts, they can be made by taking the molten raw metal and casting it in a mould. This is what happens in a foundry. Or by taking a block of solid metal and machining it using a lathe (the operation of turning, milling or grinding). Table 6 gives the French translations of the terms mentioned in this paragraph.

To know more about these processes, there is a wealth of information on the Internet and these terms can be used as keywords for searching.

Table 6. French translations of English terms in one-piece manufacturing.

| English | French |
| --- | --- |
| Lathe | *Tour* |
| Milling machine | *Fraise* |
| Grinder | *Meule* |
| One-piece | *Monobloc* |
| Mould (UK)/Mold (US) | *Moule* |
| Casting | *Coulage* |
| Cast Iron | *Fonte* |
| Foundry | *Fonderie* |

For structures that are composed of assemblies of parts, there are a variety of ways in which these are produced. By welding, bolting (or screw-assembly), riveting and push-fit or clipping. Let's concentrate on the first two.

### 4.7.2 Welding and soldering

First of all, we must explain that in French, there is a word *soudure* which can be translated as "welding". However, it can also be translated as "soldering", (and in the field of optical fibre technology as "splicing"). So what is the difference between welding and soldering?

Welding is a process in which two metallic parts are heated to a temperature such that the base metal of the two parts to be joined melts locally and the two parts brought into contact fuse together. The process may also involve the addition of a "filler metal" (*métal d'apport*) that is also melted and fills in the gap between the two metal parts. The metals thus have to be raised to a very high temperature to achieve the local melting and this is done either through oxy-fuel welding or electrical arc welding. Oxy-fuel welding involves producing a very hot flame by a combination of a flammable gas (often acetylene) and oxygen using a welding torch. The flame is run along the joint to be welded. Arc welding is done by creating an electrical arc between a welding electrode (typically made of the filler material) and the metal to be welded. Some metals (such as aluminium) are easily oxidised at the high temperatures encountered in welding and this can be avoided by creating an inert, gaseous screen around the "molten puddle" (*bain de fusion*), the locally melted region. Argon is typically used for this, hence the term "argon arc welding". MIG (Metal Inert Gas) welding is where the electrode is the filler metal that melts during the welding process. TIG (Tungsten Inert Gas) welding uses a tungsten electrode that does not melt. "Spot welding" (or "tack-welding") (*soudure par points*) is where the two parts are made to overlap and are squeezed together by a pair of electrodes. A high current induces a very small "spot" of melted metal that fuses the two parts together.

Welding is an extremely complicated process that requires highly skilled operators (welders) who have a wide knowledge of metallurgy in addition to being very dextrous in applying the procedure, using equipment that is generally very bulky. Because of this, some welding processes are automated and are done by machines. This essentially involves the electrical arc welding process with automatic feed of the filler metal if used. To give you an idea of the complexity of this subject, a translation that we did on welder training involved 54,000 words on Powerpoint slides. We were impressed!

Soldering (and brazing) is a process where two metals are joined by the application of a filler metal (solder) into the gap between the two metals, creating the joint by being melted, but the base metal is NOT melted. Soldering is used extensively in the electronics industry for joining copper wires/strips using a low melting point material (the solder) heated by a "soldering iron". In the old days, solder was lead-based but now it is tin-based for reasons of health and safety.

Soldering is also used for joining copper parts in plumbing for example. Here the solder is silver-based and this is called "silver soldering" or more commonly "brazing". The temperature necessary for melting the filler metal is much higher in this case (but not high enough to melt the base metal) and this is achieved using a "blowtorch" (*chalumeau*). As in welding, there is a need to avoid oxidation and this is achieved by coating the parts to be brazed with a flux paste that melts, creating a protective layer on the joint.

In the above we have talked about joining metal parts together but "welding" is also used for joining plastic parts together, here the temperature needed for the local melting being much lower of course and there is no need for filler materials.

---

**Machine Translation Error 3**

*au droit des soudures*

was translated as:

"required by weld law"

---

*(Continued)*

*(Continued)*

> where in fact it should have been
>
> > "at the welds".
>
> This expression
>
> > *au droit de*
>
> is frequently used in French documents and probably incorrectly. It is often mistranslated as:
>
> > "to the right of"
>
> when in fact it means
>
> > "perpendicular to"
>
> or more simply
>
> > "at".
>
> The word *droit* of course also means "law", but not in this context.

### 4.7.3 *Bolted (screwed) assemblies*

The problem with a welded assembly is that once produced it is difficult to take apart. Thus, systems where parts may need to be replaced (such as in an automobile) are generally assembled using fasteners (bolts, nuts, washers, screws, etc.).[8] First of all, what is the difference between a "bolt" and a "screw"? Well, a bolt is used to hold parts together, passing through unthreaded holes, the assembly being completed by "nuts" and "washers". A screw fits into a hole that has already been threaded using a "tap" (or in the case of a "self-tapping screw", it makes its own thread). The spiral thread on the screw itself has been produced using a "dye" that cuts around a metal stem or rod just as a "tap" cuts a spiral thread in a hole.

---

[8] One sometimes sees the word "fixation" used by engineers (not working in their own language) when the correct term is "fastening". A "fixation" is a state of mind where one is fascinated by someone or something.

Things are a lot more complicated in French. When doing a lot of translations concerning trains, we were always surprised to find that the term *vis* ("screw" in English) was used even though the parts referred to were large. One tends to think of screws as being relatively small objects while bolts are substantial in size. So why did the engineer use the word *vis* instead of *boulon* ("bolt")? In fact the latter translation is not strictly correct for French is a language of engineers. The French engineering vocabulary is perhaps richer than that in English. A *boulon* actually refers to the bolt + nut assembly. As stated above, a bolt needs to be fitted with a "nut" (*ecrou*) in order to assemble parts together. A screw in general does not need the nut (although "machine screws" do use nuts to complete the fastening). Because of the presence of the nut, some bolts are not threaded completely up to the bolt head (the stem can be smooth for some of the way down towards the threaded section). In this case the exact French term is *corps de boulon*, though we have never actually seen it used. A "screw" (*vis*) is completely threaded up to the head. There we have an exact definition of a *vis*. Never assume you know, even for the simplest screw!

So, should we have used the term "bolt" instead of "screw"? Probably.[9] Actually, apart from linguistics, things are not so simple for there are bolts that are used to screw into "blind holes". I.e., there is no nut… For a full discussion of this point, see: https://www.lavis-serie.fr/blog/21/quelle-est-la-difference-entre-boulon-ecrou-.html.

The tools used for tightening these fasteners are "screwdrivers" (*tournevis*) for screws and "spanners (UK)/wrenches (US)" (*clés*) for nuts and bolts. More specific types of the latter are "socket spanners/socket wrenches" which have a ratchet (*cliquet*) handle and are fitted with sockets (*douilles*). Often the latter are tightened to a specific value of torque using a "torque spanner (UK)/torque wrench (US)"

---

[9] Bolt = a screw-like metal object without a point, used with a nut to fasten things together (https://dictionary.cambridge.org/dictionary/english/bolt). *Boulon = Tige de fer filetée, ronde ou prismatique, comportant une tête et un écrou et servant à relier entre elles des pièces de bois ou de métal* (https://www.cnrtl.fr/definition/boulon).

(*clé dynanomètrique*) and this value is kept fixed by the application of a "thread-locking compound" (*frein-filet*). A method of ensuring that a nut and bolt set has not loosened is by marking the nut and bolt using "Ecrimetal". If this marking is seen to be shifted, then loosening has occurred.

Nuts and bolt heads generally have a hexagonal form though certain types can have a cylindrical head with a hexagonal imprint. This is designed to be fitted with an "Allen key" (*clé Allen*). Screws have various types of imprint that can be a straight "slot" (*fente*) that is turned by a "flat screwdriver" (*tournevis plat*). The problem with this design is that the screwdriver easily slides out of the slot so other types of imprint have been designed in various shapes such as a cross (Phillips screw), a star (Torx) or a type we have only seen in Canada which has a square imprint (Robinson screw).

If you really need to understand the different designations of nuts and bolts, there is a wealth of information to be found at: https://www.fastenermart.com/understanding-metric-fasteners.html. If you want to quickly learn more about all these different mechanical engineering techniques and objects, a very useful website is: https://monroeengineering.com/blog.

### 4.7.4 Standards

This is a field that a scientist may not be very familiar with, science by its very nature being the quest for the new and unexpected. But when you get away from the academic world, and into the "real" world if you like, you do not want the unexpected. You want to know how a machine will work, what is the right material to use for designing the inside of a railway compartment, what size of windows should you be putting in your house, how to conduct a test of an automobile so that it is accepted by the community and the government, etc. In other words, in the real world, you like things to be standardised so that you can have confidence in them. This is where "standards" (*normes*) come in. There are professional organisations that establish standards or specifications for products, processes, ways of doing things, etc.

Frequently in technical translations and in particular in engineering, you will see these standards referred to. Most well known are the ISO standards which apply to businesses or organisations that have been audited by the International Standards Organisation (ISO) to make sure that they conform to the standards of activity established by this organisation. (Of course, there are other such organisations and in particular national ones). For example, the 9001 standard refers to "quality" and the "quality control" procedures applied by the organisation. If you want products tested for their chemical or engineering properties, you have this done by a laboratory. How can you know if the laboratory is trustworthy and that you can have confidence in the results? One way to be sure is if the laboratory has acquired ISO 9001 certification. This is desirable but not compulsory. Other standards are compulsory and for example the behaviour of materials that will be incorporated into a railcar, an automobile, or an airplane must conform to accepted standards established by professional bodies. In this way you know that these products are safe.

Often, these standards are referred to in technical documents with their reference number and the corresponding description. For example:

NF EN 16729-3

*Application ferroviaires — Infrastructure — Essais non destructifs sur les rails de voie — Partie 3 : exigences pour l'identification des défauts internes et de surface des rails —*

"Railway applications — Infrastructure — Non-destructive testing on rails in track — Part 3: requirements for identifying internal and surface rail defects — ".

The best advice here is not to translate the text or title of the standard yourself, but to look it up on the Internet and take their version directly. This is not to say that the translation you find is strictly correct but at least it is consistent from one document to another. As you can see in the example above, "rails in track" does not seem like the correct translation for *rails de voie* ("track rails").

For French standards, the website where you can get this information is the AFNOR (*Association Française de Normalisation*) boutique: https://www.boutique.afnor.org/, where you can search for standards by their reference number in French or English. It would be nice to obtain the actual text of these standards, but they are for sale and frankly cost a fortune. Selling standards is a very lucrative business because if they exist, the professionals who must use them must buy them.

### 4.7.5 *Testing*

When a structure, a piece of equipment or an assembly is produced, it often needs to undergo testing and this can involve Non-Destructive Testing (NDT) or Destructive Testing. The former is typically for a part or structure that will subsequently be used while the latter is for a prototype. NDT can entail ultrasonic testing, X-ray radiography, gamma radiography, neutron radiography and often *ressuage* which is translated as "dye-penetrant testing".

---

**Machine Translation Error 4**

*perméabilité des matériaux aux ultrasons*

was translated as

"permeability of ultrasonic materials"

but there is no such thing as an ultrasonic material. This is a misinterpretation of the term *à* (here, the plural form *aux*) which is often used to indicate that the following word is an adjective. It should of course have been:

"permeability of materials to ultrasound".

---

### 4.7.6 *Special terminology*

One of the problems encountered when doing mechanical engineering translations is that often you come across terms that make no sense. Some years back we had a translation concerning the testing of a large turbine shaft and in the text, it said that a *lunette* was used for

**Figure 12.** A steady-rest. Copyright © Richter Lünetten, licensed under CC BY-SA 2.0 DE.

this test.[10] In French, *lunettes* are "spectacles" or, more colloquially, "eye-glasses", in other words what you wear to see better. But a *lunette* can also be a lens of an optical apparatus or even a gunsight. We weren't happy with either of these although you could imagine that the second choice might make some sense for lining up the turbine shaft. A bit more investigation, however, finally led to the correct choice. It was a "steady-rest", a bit like that shown in Figure 12.

This is a device used on a lathe for supporting the end of a long shaft while it is machined. This is just an example of how one can be easily mistaken if you do not analyse the problem carefully. Another term that was used in this text was the word *coupon*. As everyone knows, a coupon is what you take to the supermarket to get a price reduction. But in this case no. Again, you had to really read the text to understand what was being said. In this context, a *coupon* is a "test-piece" of metal (often a weld-coupon) that was going to be analysed to determine its physical characteristics.

---

[10] See also the discussion of *lunette* in Section 4.5.

A very strange term that appears sometimes in documents regarding an industrial process that may involve mechanical engineering or other processes is:

*Document Unique.*

The obvious translation would be:

"single document",

or

"sole document"

or even

"unique document".

But this is wrong in this context. The actual translation is

"Risk Evaluation"

or

"Professional Risk Evaluation".

This is really not obvious though the complete term should be: *DUERP — Document Unique d'Evaluation des Risques Professionnel* (something like "The one and only document of professional risk evaluation"!).

---

**Machine Translation Error 5**

In a translation that we worked on, the sentence:

*Les dispositions doivent être prises pour <u>assurer l'absence de condensation</u> sur les pièces jusqu'à l'application du système de peinture.*

was machine translated as:

"Provisions must be taken to ensure that the parts are not condensed until the paint system is applied."

(Continued)

> But this makes no sense! The correct translation is:
>
> "Provisions must be made to <u>ensure that no condensation forms</u> on the parts until the paint system is applied."

---

**Machine Translation Error 6**

The following sentence appeared in a translation involving a moulding process where a liquid substance was poured into a mould to subsequently harden. However, for technical reasons, the cooling had to be handled carefully. Thus there was the sentence:

*afin de maintenir une température intérieure minimale.*

This was translated as

"to keep the interior temperature to a minimum"

suggesting that the interior temperature should not be allowed to rise above a low value. This did not make sense in the context of the document. It should actually have been translated as:

"to maintain a minimum interior temperature"

i.e., to maintain the temperature at a minimum temperature during the process.

---

### 4.7.7 Exercises

Find the correct translations for:

1. *Magnétoscopie (MT)*
2. *Mep UT*
3. *TTAS*
4. *CND*
5. *Rondelle griffe*
6. *Pas de pèlerin soudage*
7. *Chaude de retrait*

8. *Pièce martyre*
9. *TOFD UT PA*

## 4.8 Construction

This is a major area for technical translation, and it covers a lot of territory. Building specifications, geological surveys of future building sites, building fittings, tunnelling, road construction and many other topics. It can often involve some legal aspects and we shall come back to that later. After having received a number of jobs in this area and having spent much time searching for terminology on the Internet, we decided to invest in the king of dictionaries in this area: The Dicobat Dictionaries (Figure 13).

This is a superb reference with many illustrated examples, explaining not only the terms in French but also giving their English equivalents. And this is very important for this area has a very rich vocabulary. Whether it is roofing parts, concrete structures, excavations, locks or

Figure 13.   The Dicobat dictionaries for construction terminology.

door fittings, you will find what you need there. For those of you not working in French, it is very worthwhile to find the equivalent, particularly an illustrated dictionary. Just cherry picking from a range of possible terms is not good enough and if you want to appear professional, you have to know the right term. Sometimes clients will provide you with their own glossaries and this can be helpful but also a double-edged sword. It often happens that the client uses the wrong term and you know this. But if you decide that you know better, be prepared for complaints. We have worked for many years with one particular client who insists that *défaut* is translated as "failure" and not "fault". It is no good trying to change their minds as they have used this term in countless other documents.

What do you need for translating construction documents apart from a good dictionary? Basically you need knowledge in at least the following areas:

- **Buildings:** Let's say you are doing a translation about the construction of a building. Then you should know about things like the names of different walls (partition walls, pre-cast concrete walls, etc.), the names of fittings (skirting boards, plinths, lighting fixtures, electrical outlets, false ceilings), etc. Sometimes, the terms you see are not obvious. For example, a *réservation* in French is a "service sleeve" or a "box-out" in English. I.e., a hole in a wall. Large buildings are usually formed from concrete, cast into "formwork" (*coffrage*), i.e., temporary assemblies, and erected before the casting, into which concrete is poured. The concrete may be reinforced using "rebars" (*armature*), steel rods inserted into the moulds around which the concrete forms. Other words will give you pause; we were surprised to find the word *circulations* used for an office building. Reading through the text, we realised they were talking about "corridors".
- **Doors:** We once did a translation that was all about doors. This was complicated and was the first time we really had to search for illustrations to see what they were talking about. There were terms like "door leaf" (*vantail*), "door frame" (*huisserie*), "door jamb"

(*chambranle*), "lintels" (*linteaux*), "mullion" (*montant intermediaire*), "rabbet" (*refeuillement*), etc., that are very specific to this topic, some of which you might not be even familiar with in English. Here, a visual dictionary is a godsend as it will help you to understand what these items actually are or what purpose they serve.
- **Locks (*serrurie*):** obviously an important item in any construction project. Again, there is a lot of specific terminology such as "strike-plate" (*gache*), "tumbler lock" (*serrure à barillet*), "lock bolt" (*pêne*), "deadlock" (*serrure à pêne dormant*).
- **Plumbing (*plomberie*):** This is an interesting word in French for *plomb* of course means "lead" and in the past lead pipes were used for delivering water to dwellings and a plumber was the person who installed them. Generally, these terms are not so difficult though it is not always clear what the difference is between a *robinet* and a *vanne* even though you might think it is obvious. As always, if in doubt (or even if you are not in doubt), it is good to check with a technical dictionary.
- **Excavations:** now we are outside and here there are machines, possibly with "tracks" (*chenilles*) and "buckets" (*godets*), piledrivers, trenches, underground networks (water mains, gas mains), and there are roadworks with the laying of asphalt, "backfilling" (*remblais*),[11] "spoils" or "muck" (*déblais*).
- **Air treatment systems:** HVAC (Heating Ventilation, Air Conditioning), "heat pumps" (*pompes à chaleur*), etc.

As you can see, the subject is very wide and if you say that you can translate in the field of construction, you may be asked to do projects in all these areas.

Two terms that you see very regularly in French documents related to construction are *Maître d'Œuvre* (MOE) and *Maître d'Ouvrage* (MOA). This can seem confusing, but they have very different roles. The *Maître d'Œuvre* is the "Project Manager". They

---

[11] Note that *remblai* also means an "embankment".

organise the work site and are responsible for managing the different trades (*métiers*). An alternative term for them is "Building Engineer". Generally, the MOE is a person but for a large project, it could also be the design office or an architect. In essence the MOE is the person on the ground or entity who oversees the project and who delivers regular reports back to the *Maître d'Ouvrage*. Why do they do it? Because the *Maître d'Ouvrage* is the boss. It is the person, agency or company who has ordered the work to be done. In fact, a good term for MOA is "Contracting Authority" though "client" can also be used. It is good to get these two terms straight in your head for if you start looking at the Internet, you will find conflicting definitions that can confuse you.

### 4.8.1 *Exercises*

Find the correct translation for:

1. *Tel que construit (TQC)*
2. *Bon pour exécution (BPE)*
3. *Escalier helicoidal*
4. *Nomenclature*
5. *Economiste de la construction*

## 4.9 Nuclear Engineering

Translations that we have done in this field have ranged from safety plans for nuclear reactors to technical manuals on the replacement of sensors in nuclear plants and, by extension, the sterilisation of medical devices and their packaging using radioisotopes and electron accelerators. The first thing to say here is that you should have a good knowledge of how a nuclear reactor works, what are the risks incurred with reactor operation and radioisotope handling, etc. Indeed, a solid knowledge of physics is a prerequisite along with at least a general knowledge of the issues involved with nuclear power. Whatever your feelings about nuclear power (and we as physicists have a positive view

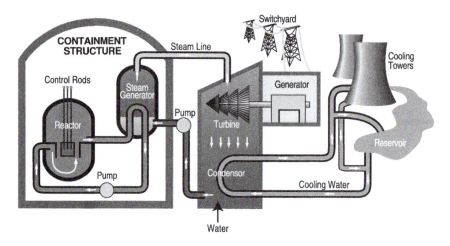

**Figure 14.** Schematic diagram of a nuclear power plant. Public domain.

of it), this is a major industry with a long history behind it. This means that there is a very extensive vocabulary that has to be mastered.

Basically, a nuclear reactor (Figure 14) operates by having bundles of slightly enriched uranium fuel rods (*crayons* in French) contained in a reactor vessel through which a coolant (usually water) flows. There are several types of rods:

- "Fuel rod" — *crayon combustible*
- "Control rod" — *crayon absorbant*
- "Thimble plug" — *crayon bouchon*
- "Source rod" — *crayon source*
- "Burnable poison rod" — *crayon de poison consommable*

and these can be arranged in "clusters" (*grappes*).

The coolant serves as a moderator for slowing down the neutrons produced by the nuclear fission reaction, and the heat released in this reaction heats the moderator/coolant which generates steam that turns a turbine connected to an alternator for the generation of electricity. The nuclear reaction begins when control rods made of materials with high neutron capture abilities are withdrawn from the fuel bundles, allowing free neutrons coming from the fuel to react with more fuel nuclei to generate a so-called fission chain reaction, liberating energetic particles (more neutrons and fission fragments), their kinetic energy being converted to heat by collision with the moderator/coolant liquid. The rate of this reaction is controlled by moving the control rods in and out as needed.

There are different versions of the technology (boiling water reactors (BWR), pressurised water reactors (PWR), Candu reactors, etc.) but the key elements are basically the same. The issues that you encounter in translations often concern the operating procedures for safety systems, the response procedures in case of incidents, the most serious of course being a loss-of-coolant accident (LOCA). Environmental issues are of great importance, particularly if there are accidental releases of gases or liquids, and of course there is the major question of spent fuel storage. Like aeronautics, there is a whole glossary of language behind this technology that is relatively standard, and an Internet search is the best way to check the right translation for any given term. Like any other area however, your translation is only as good as your understanding of what you are translating.

A particularly impressive document that we use is the *Réacteurs à Eau Pressurisée: Ilôts Nucléaires Lexique Français Anglais des Termes Techniques* ("Pressurised Water Reactors: Nuclear Islands") that was produced by Framatome, a company that operates 68 nuclear reactors. This document contains 15,000 terms related to this industry. If you are going to do a lot of translating in this area, it is worth investing in, though your client may be able to let you have a copy (Figure 15).[12] For other languages, you must search to see what resources are available to you to help you with this topic.

A recent translation that we did regarding nuclear safety and operating practices was particularly challenging for it contained a virtual myriad of acronyms, almost all of which had no English equivalent. Many of these referred to job functions. What does a translator do in this case? A lot depends on what the client wants. The ideal situation is to ask for a glossary of acronyms so that you know what they mean,

---

[12] We actually found a PDF of this on the Internet but eventually decided to purchase the actual book which turned out to be a very wise decision.

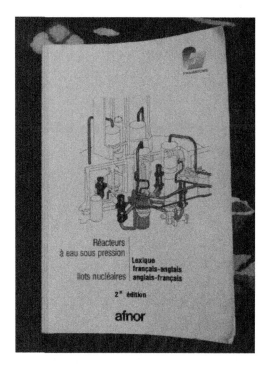

Figure 15. The Framatome nuclear technology glossary (French/English).

at least. Sometimes clients want the acronyms to be transferred to the target document as is. Other want the acronyms to be translated into text if there is no English equivalent.

What we generally do is to copy the acronym from the source to the target and then (in square brackets) give the English translation of the corresponding French term. If the client does not like this, they can always erase it. In the particular instance found in this nuclear translation, what we did was to convert the acronym directly into English text. The feeling was that at least the reader would understand what was written and to heck with the gobbledygook[13] of acronym spaghetti. (I think you can see we don't like acronyms).

---

[13] Gobbledygook — an incomprehensible mixture of words.

One of the problems with acronyms is that if you look them up on the Internet, you are quite likely to find corresponding text that comes from a quite different area and so is completely inappropriate. This is what can be called a major error.

---

**Machine Translation Error 7**

The following sentence:

*En cours d'opération normale, l'une des deux cellules est l'Actif et l'autre est le Passif en attente pour une reprise à chaud en cas de défaillance de l'Actif.*

was translated as if it were a business document where an *Actif* is an "Asset" and a *Passif* is a "Liability", thus:

"In the normal course of business, one of the two cells is the Asset and the other is the Liabilities waiting for a hot recovery in the event of a failure of the Asset."

This should of course have been:

"Under normal operation, one of the two cells is the Active and the other is the Passive waiting for an immediate takeover in the event of a failure of the Active."

---

**Machine Translation Error 8**

During the operation of a nuclear reactor, there are conditions where boron has to be added to slow down the nuclear reaction. This is because boron is a strong absorber of neutrons that are the initiators of a chain reaction. This can be done by insertion of control rods containing boron or via injection of boron into the reactor cooling circuit. The term

*eau borée*

should not, however, be translated as:

"bored water"

but rather as:

"borated water".

> **Machine Translation Error 9**
>
> *Les accidents sans arrêt*
>
> should not be translated as:
>
> "Non-stop accidents"
>
> but rather as:
>
> "Accidents without shut-down".

### 4.9.1 *Exercises*

Find the correct translation for:

1. *Tranche*
2. *Anthropogammétrie*
3. *Réfrigérant atmosphérique*
4. *Essai hydraulique*

## 4.10 Renewable Energy

We are living in a different world now and never has it been more stark than when it comes to energy. Coal, oil, gas, petrol and diesel are seen with a baneful eye by many people and certainly some of them merit this consideration. The City of London banned the use of coal for home heating in 1956 because of the number of deaths that results from the heavy fogs it induced. Nowadays, air pollution, which people have been concerned about for years if not decades, is now recognised as just one element in the argument against burning these "fossil fuels", fuels that were produced naturally from the decay of vegetation over a period of millions of years. Fuels that will never be produced again in in the probable lifespan of humanity. The real fear now is that the carbon dioxide produced by the fossil fuel industry (from upstream production to downstream use) will eventually lead to the phenomenon of global warming and climate change. We may already be seeing indications of the latter, though separating man-made effects from natural ones is a subject of great dispute.

Whatever your opinion on these matters, one thing is clear and that is Renewable Energy is becoming a serious alternative to fossil fuel burning for the production of energy and, in particular, energy in the form of electricity. Hence, there is a lot of translating to be done.

First of all, what is renewable energy? Basically, there are two kinds. One type is where mechanical energy is generated from the conversion of natural fluid motion. This is most usually thought of in terms of wind power, with the "wind turbines" (*éoliennes*) either individually situated or concentrated in "wind farms" (*parcs éoliens*). What we used to call "windmills", a frequent sight in old Dutch paintings, are now giant monsters with vanes that can be 200 metres in length (Figure 16), turning slowly in the wind and driving turbine generators through a gearbox system. These devices convert the wind energy into mechanical rotation by means of the vanes of the device that act like giant propellers, though acting in reverse. Instead of a turbine engine driving a propeller, like in a modern airplane, these propellers drive a turbine. Their induced mechanical rotational energy is in turn converted into electrical energy. These wind turbines are

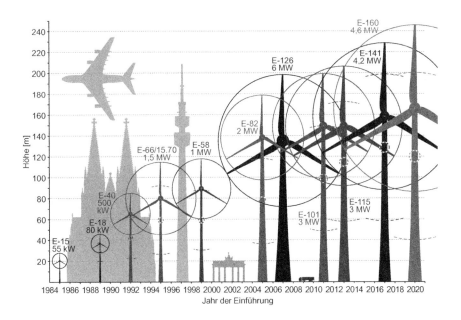

**Figure 16.    Increase in size of wind turbines over the years. Public domain.**

typically connected to the electrical grid and their operation is controlled by "operators" (*exploitants*) and the companies who "operate" (*exploitent*) the system. The feeding of energy into the "electrical grid" (*réseau électrique*) is controlled by the grid operator, generally a national organisation or one operating under the auspices of the government.

Wind is not the only "fluid" that can be used for the production of mechanical and thus electrical energy. Like air, water is a fluid in constant motion whether in the form of waves, tides or ocean currents. Tidal power has been used to produce energy, in particular at the *station marémotrice* ("tidal power station") near Saint Malo in western France (Figure 17). This requires a very special environment and thus, up until now, has not been adopted on a large scale elsewhere.[14]

**Figure 17. The tidal power plant in Saint Malo. Copyright © Dani 7C3, licensed under CC BY 2.5.**

---

[14] There is a small power station in Canada and another in Russia.

New technologies are being developed seeking to capture mechanical energy from "wave surges" (*houles*). This is called *énergie houlomotrice* in French and "wave energy" in English. Another system seeks to capture the energy from ocean currents using *hydroliennes* or "flow-driven turbines". These marine-based technologies have many challenges (corrosion, clogging, effects on marine life) and so are at a much earlier state of maturity than the wind-based systems. It is quite possible, however, to find translations in these areas, particularly in the form of Requests for Quotation (RFQ or *Consultation* in French) and technical specifications and contracts.

Another form of renewable energy is sunlight and this is a technology that has seen enormous growth, ever since the development of solar panels used in the space race in the second half of the $20^{th}$ century. Solar farms are where vast arrays of solar panels are installed in a free area, capturing the energy from sunlight and converting it directly into electricity. This technology uses the photoelectric effect (for which Albert Einstein won his Nobel Prize) and this process occurs in photoelectric cells (*cellules photovoltaïques*). Alternatively, small-scale systems can be installed on the roofs of buildings (houses, farm buildings, factories, etc.) and the electricity thus generated can be used either in-house or it can be sold to the local electricity companies for injection into the national grid. This process requires a sophisticated energy sharing system where energy demand is matched with available supply. These photoelectric cells are made of silicon semiconductor materials with various dopants to produce their electrical conversion functionality. Again, translations in this area often concern contracts and specifications.

The Internet is a very rich source of information on all these areas we have mentioned and before tackling a translation, it is very worthwhile to do a search for this information to get a feel for the technology and the terminology used. You cannot do a good job of translating if you do not understand the material you are dealing with so the translator should bear this in mind when accepting any job.

Hydroelectric power also falls under the title of renewable energy, since it is produced by the movement of water through turbines for the generation of energy, and the amount of water available for this ultimately comes from natural precipitation whether in the form of rain or snow. Unlike wind power, ocean power and solar power, this is an old technology dating back to the early days of the use of electricity and so we have devoted a separate section to it (Section 4.11).

Burning wood can also be considered as renewable energy and one can perhaps think of it as being carbon neutral as the trees forming the wood absorb carbon dioxide which is then released when the wood is burned. This is very popular with many people who feel that burning wood in stoves is something ecological. After all, you can also plant new trees and renew the source. Unfortunately, burning wood is far from being environmentally friendly as it releases quite a cocktail of Volatile Organic Carbon and Polycyclic Aromatic Hydrocarbon pollutants that might smell nice but that are not necessarily good for the environment. In addition, wood-burning stoves are typically not optimised in terms of combustion efficiency to the same extent as, let's say, oil or gas furnaces, so although one can think of oneself as an eco-friendly citizen, the reality may be far from the truth. Again, it is worth checking out the Internet sources on this subject if, for example, you are given the job of translating a brochure for a wood-burning stove.

Certainly, renewable energy is here to stay and if you have started your career in translation on the basis of your knowledge of the oil and gas industry, you might consider reconverting yourself into this domain.

> Just while we are talking of electricity, we were doing a translation from French to English a few days ago about a company who had developed a method for separating waste plastics using the *turbo-électrique* effect. This seemed strange as we had never heard of such a thing. The article was in fact part of a newsletter and had been written by a journalist. We decided to check the website of the company who had invented this technique, and sure enough, they were using the "tribo-electric" effect and not the "turbo-electric" effect. Tribo-electricity is the generation of an electric charge by friction or contact. We mention this because when you are translating, sometimes the source document contains errors, especially if written by someone without a science background. You have to keep awake when doing technical translation!

> **Machine Translation Error 10**
>
> *Personne n'est à l'abri d'un oubli ou d'un instant d'inattention*
>
> is translated as:
>
> "No one is safe from oblivion or a moment of inattention"
>
> instead of:
>
> "No one is safe from forgetfulness or a moment of inattention".

### 4.10.1 *Exercises*

Find the correct translation for:

1. *Poste de transformation électrique*
2. *Evacuation d'énergie*

## 4.11 Hydroelectric Power and Hydraulic Engineering

This can be classified as renewable energy, but it is far from being new. Indeed, Man has been converting the potential and kinetic energy of water into mechanical energy for centuries. Whether by using a fast-flowing stream to turn a water wheel or a dam to control the flow through an electrical turbine generator, this is a source of energy that has many attractions, though sometimes accompanied by environmental consequences and even risks for public safety. This means that there is a whole language devoted to this subject and to the closely associated subject of hydraulic engineering. By the latter, we mean the use and management of water resources. While the dam shown in Figure 18 is specifically created for the production of electricity, other dams are used to control water flow in valleys or regions where flooding is likely to occur during periods of excessive precipitation and melting of snow.

In the figure, we see that the dam (the barrier structure) is used to create a *réservoir*. Normally we would translate this word as "tank" but not in this case. The area surrounding the reservoir that collects

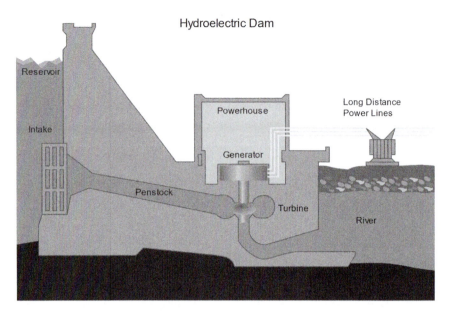

Figure 18. Schematic diagram of a hydroelectric dam. Copyright © Tennessee Valley Authority, licensed under CC BY 2.5.

the water (from rain, snow, etc.) is known as the "catchment area" or "watershed" (*bassin versant*). The water is allowed to flow through an intake and then down a sloping pipe called a "penstock" (*conduite forcée* or *vanne de tête*). The flow of water through the intake can be controlled by a type of valve (not shown in figure) with the particular term "sluice gate" (*vanne*). The water then passes through the turbine before being discharged downstream into the river through a "tailrace" (*canal de fuite*).

(JBAM) While writing this section of the book, I had a terrible feeling that I made a mistake in a translation I did some months back concerning a system of control for a hydroelectric power station (*usine*). This was mainly about the Supervisory Control And Data Acquisition which is used to regulate the power output from the station. Obviously, this is something that is critical to the efficient operation of a power plant supplying the electricity grid (*réseau*). Several times the term *vannage* was used, which in English is usually translated as "winnowing" (the operation of separating wheat grains from chaff (husks) under the action of wind). In this context it should have been "sluicing", i.e., the action of regulating the flow of water by means of adjusting the level of opening of sluice gates in the lower part of the dam. What is confusing is that the word winnowing actually does appear in some documents regarding hydroelectric power, but it refers to the separation of fine silt from coarse silt particles under the action of flowing water. This is an example where one can be fooled into using the wrong terminology because one is not in the specific context.

Hydraulic engineering covers a broad field as one is also called upon to do translations about valves and pumps for example. The former subject can be very confusing for in French, the general term for valves is *robinetterie*, while in school you learn that *robinet* is a "tap". In fact, these terms seem to be used interchangeably in engineering documents. Often there is a qualification on the type of valve that is referred to. For example:

- *Soupape* = "check valve", "safety valve" or "pressure relief valve" (sometimes the term simply means "valve")
- *Vanne à boisseau sphérique* = "ball valve"
- *Vanne tiroir* = "gate valve"

and as we have seen above:

- *Vanne* (in the water management context) = "sluice gate".

Given the widespread use of valves in the industry, you can expect to come across documents where these are discussed in detail and so you will be faced with a lot of searching to get exactly the right term. Often this information can be found on the websites of valve manufacturers or wholesalers/retailers and if you happen to find a multilingual site, cross-referencing can lead you to the exact term. One such site is http://www.flowserve/ that gives extensive information on valves and pumps, but there are many more. Here again, much of the translator's job involves Internet searching to get the right term.

Talking about pumps, here you will find terminology that is specific to the field and we just want to mention one particular term and that is "head". For example, a characteristic of a pump is the

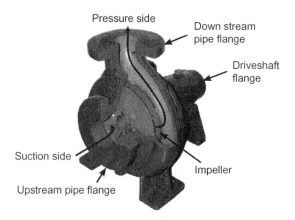

**Figure 19.** Parts of a centrifugal pump. Copyright © Fantagu (edited by sunspeanzler), licensed under CC BY-SA 3.0.

"Net Positive Suction Head" (NPSH), which can be qualified as "Net Positive Suction Head Available (NPSHA — the absolute pressure at the suction port of the pump) or "Net Positive Suction Head Required" (NPSHR — the minimum pressure required at the suction port to avoid cavitation).

To understand this we must introduce a little mathematics, namely the Bernoulli equation, which states that in a frictionless flow mechanical energy is conserved and this can be written as:

$$p_1 + \frac{1}{2}\rho v_1^2 + \rho g H_1 = p_2 + \frac{1}{2}\rho v_2^2 + \rho g H_2$$

where the second term is the kinetic energy of the fluid with density $\rho$ and the third term (involving height) is the potential energy of the fluid at a relative height $H$ ($g$ is the acceleration of gravity). This is one of the most important equations in fluid mechanics, equivalent to the conservation of energy in particle mechanics. We can play with this equation by dividing each term by $\rho g$ to get:

$$\frac{p_1}{\rho g} + \frac{v_1^2}{2g} + H_1 = \frac{p_2}{\rho g} + \frac{v_2^2}{2g} + H_2.$$

The reason we do this is that now, each term is expressed in the units of height (centimetres, metres, inches, feet, etc.) And we call these heights "heads". Thus:

- $\frac{p}{\rho g}$ is called the "Pressure Head"
- $\frac{v^2}{2g}$ is called the "Velocity Head"
- $H$ is called the "Potential Head"

Fluids (i.e., liquids or gases) flowing through pipework can lose energy when they encounter bends, changes of pipework cross-section, rough walls, the onset of turbulence, and an increase in the Reynold's number ($\rho v D/\mu$), where $\mu$ is the viscosity of the fluid and $D$ is a characteristic length. For a pipe, $D$ is the diameter. Turbulence is a subject still not understood by physicists from a fundamental point of view so our understanding of it is based on "empirical" studies, i.e., studies based on experimental measurements. From these studies we can formulate a concept of how much energy is lost when the fluid flows though the pipework by adding another term to Bernoulli's equation, thus:

$$\frac{p_1}{\rho g} + \frac{v_1^2}{2g} + H_1 = \frac{p_2}{\rho g} + \frac{v_2^2}{2g} + H_2 + \Delta H$$

where the term $\Delta H$ (delta H) means there is a difference in H. A difference in "head".

There is a specific name for $\Delta H$ that is often encountered in translations involving the movement of fluids through pumps and valves: "Head Loss", which the French call *Perte de Charge*. JBAM taught Fluid Mechanics for many years in France and would tell his students that the French didn't like this term as it reminded them too much of the *guillotine*!

A couple of other things could be mentioned here. Often in engineering texts in French, one sees the term *Delta* specifically mentioned but this is not really done in English so it is better to replace this by "Difference", even though an engineer would probably understand if you used "Delta".[15]

Another concept worth mentioning is cavitation, which we saw above in the explanation of the term "Net Positive Suction Head Required". This is a destructive phenomenon that can and does cause damage to pumps and most particularly to ship propellers (or pump impellers). We can understand it by looking at Bernoulli's equation. To keep everything balanced on both sides of the equation, when the velocity increases, i.e., $v_2$ becomes greater than $v_1$ ($v_2 > v_1$), to compensate for the equilibrium the pressure in the fluid $p_2$ must decrease so that $p_2$ is less than $p_1$ ($p_2 < p_1$) with the density $\rho$ and $g$ both being constant. Every fluid has a partial pressure (the pressure of the fluid vapour), and when this pressure becomes equal to the local pressure, vapour bubbles form. This is what happens when the kettle boils. The same occurs within the fluid if the local pressure drops, so bubbles form around a propeller. The problem is that when the bubbles burst, they release a lot of energy that is transferred to the material of the propeller (or impeller) and this causes the damage.

We have been talking about inequalities, namely "<" for less than and ">" for greater than. It should be noted that the terms "greater than or equal to" ($\geq$) and "less than or equal to" ($\leq$) are standard scientific, mathematical, and engineering terminology and should be used where appropriate for translating *supérieur ou égal à* or *inférieur ou égal à* in French and not "no greater than" or "no more than".

### 4.11.1 Exercises

Find the correct translation for:

1. *Electrovanne*
2. *Caloporteur*
3. *Structures émergées et structures immergées*
4. *Vanne guillotine*

---

[15] By the way, here we are speaking another language called "mathematics" where the Greek letter "Delta" is the symbol for the difference. (It is actually an operator). Let's leave it here.

## 4.12 Insurance

We have found that actually one of the most interesting areas of technical translation is insurance. Not the writing of insurance policies and terms and conditions of these policies. This is the domain of legal and financial translation and you really have to be an expert in these subjects to be able to render acceptable translations.

What is really interesting are the reports of accident investigations by insurance companies. In these investigations insurance personnel visit the site of the accident and evaluate the damage, how much it will cost to replace the equipment, buildings, etc., and how much loss of income the victim will suffer because of the accident. The victim may have already estimated these figures and the insurance company will decide, according to its investigation, if these figures are reasonable or if they are greatly inflated. In other words, if the estimated costs actually refer to the damage done or if they are the result of subsequent "upgrading" as we saw in one report. The difference in the victim's estimated costs and those agreed by the insurance company can be quite (or even very) wide in some cases but the reasons for these differences have to be well explained to avoid subsequent legal action.

In the language that I have used in these two paragraphs, only one word is in fact used in these reports, that are structured in many ways like patents, in that there must be no room for ambiguity in the terminology used. Thus, the expert who performs the investigation is called an:

> "adjuster"

for it is this person who will "adjust" the amount of the insurance payment to the:

> "policy holder".

The insurance company that holds the insurance policy is the:

> "insurer".

This company may or may not be responsible for the final payment to the client (victim) as the damage may have been caused by equipment that failed and so the manufacturer or supplier of this equipment may be the:

"liable party".

The investigation itself is called an:

"appraisal".

There is a term used in French that is very confusing:

*Expertise contradictoire.*

What this means in fact is that the "appraisal visit or inspection" is made in the presence of all the parties concerned (*parties prenantes*):

"the stakeholders".

These are representatives of the company or entity that has suffered the damage, their insurer, the adjuster, representative of the company that made the equipment that failed, their insurer, etc. etc. The events leading to this event could be a fire, a storm, etc., and in French this is called

*sinistre.*

While normally this term refers to an accident, in this insurance context the term in English is:

"loss".

Because of the accident, the insured party (the victim) has suffered a loss. And there are two types of losses:

*dommage direct* and *dommage indirect.*

The first is the damage caused directly to the building, equipment, etc., the replacement of which should be covered by the insurance. In English this is:

"property damage",

i.e., damage caused to the property belonging to the insured party. However, as a result of the unavailability of this "property", the victim will not be able to render services or manufacture products — this is what the second French term refers to. A good translation for this is:

"business interruption".

The appraisal will result in the production of a:

*rapport d'évaluation*

which is an

"appraisal report",

in which the:

*constats*

or

"findings"

are described along with:

"perspectives",

i.e., what will happen as a result of this report and possibly:

*recours à poursuivre,*

meaning

"recourse to be pursued".

We have insisted on discussing these terms because these reports are legal in nature and as we have stated above, there must be no ambiguity in their use. Indeed, this is one of the key issues in technical translation. One's goal is not to produce a literary masterpiece, using flowery language and great erudition. The goal is to produce a document that is accurate and that reports the facts in as clear a fashion as possible, while adhering to the style expected in the target language (which is not necessarily the style of the source language).

As a technical translator, there is often the criticism that what you have produced is too "literal" or "word-for-word". This is something you have to work on, to avoid this trap while keeping to the meaning of the document. We have seen the suggestions of proofreaders that are completely inaccurate as they did not understand the context. More about that later.

## 4.13 Patents

First of all, what are patents? Patents are legal documents that describe inventions in great detail. Detail that is sufficient to completely and exactly describe the invention so that as stated, it can only be used/produced by the patent holder or by an assignee (the person or entity that the inventor has assigned the patent to) or to a licensee (the person or entity that pays a licence for the use of the invention or the right to reproduce/manufacture it).

So let's say you have been asked to translate a patent. Here are a few words of advice. Firstly, do not try anything fancy when translating them. Oh sorry, we meant, when translating "same", or better, when translating "said patents". Do you feel this is going wrong? Very wrong? Take a deep breath and read a patent. If you translate from English, take a few breaths and maybe do some meditation exercise before reading the whole patent. You will start off being surprised, and it will not get any easier or more pleasant. When finished, you will feel relief and, well, the rest depends on your personality and education. You might politely refuse the job. Just because everything you learn you should not do when writing, you do here. But if you accept it, keep in mind that it is about accuracy and accuracy alone. You will most certainly get instructions, maybe a guide, and even the translation of sentences with legal meaning. You will be told not to use pronouns and repeat "said" to make sure that you refer to the same specific object you have already mentioned. Why are patents so unclear then?

You repeat and repeat the same thing over and over again. You don't use any pronouns to avoid repeating a word and you use ridiculously long sentences to keep one idea in one sentence. Marcel Proust would be jealous! There is a style that you have to adhere to because if you do not use the appropriate style, you could render the patent valueless. We have heard stories of how a single word in a patent was incorrect, and this meant that the whole patent application process had to be repeated. And patent filing can be a very expensive processes involving lawyers, resubmission, and possibly subsequent counter-claims by competitors.

Fortunately, there is no shortage of information on patents and patent drafting and you can follow these guidelines while formulating your translation. The World International Patent Organisation has manuals in English, French, Spanish, Arabic and Chinese (see for instance the French version at https://www.wipo.int/publications/fr/details.jsp?id=297&plang=FR). The European Patent Office also has a section called "Preparing and filing a European patent application" (see https://e-courses.epo.org/wbts/htgaep_en/index.html) where you can find examples of very well-written patents in the "Drafting the technical application documents" sub-section. This information is available in English, French and German.

So, anybody could learn how to write a clear, elegant, concise patent. In principle….

We were never asked to translate a patent application for filing. This is really for the specialists. We always translated patents that have already been awarded. Having said that, one of us (AIFM) has translated literally thousands of patent reports where style has to follow official rules insofar as the legal terminology is concerned. These reports are sent to patent applicants informing them as to whether their application has been accepted or not. The key words here are "Novelty", "Innovation" and "Industrial Application". A patent has to fulfil each of these criteria in order to be accepted and of course the patent examiner will make sure that another patent does not exist on the same subject. This is a major area of conflict and has led to patent wars. One famous patent war was between the Exxon and Mobil oil companies involving 100 and 50 patents respectively. Eventually, Exxon decided that the process was going to be too expensive, so instead it bought Mobil for about $54 billion! As you can see, patents are very precious documents.

But let's say that you do accept the challenge and you start the translation. Again, the key thing here is accuracy and you must reproduce the original text exactly as stated. There is no room for literary style that could potentially feed the wrong information. Wade through the document, and this can be a very onerous task given those long sentences, and understand what is being said. Now we mean, really understand.

So, there are a few rules you should follow when translating a patent, let us assume, from English to a target language:

- Read the whole patent
- Make a summary for yourself, in your own words, to see if you really understood it
- Extract the relevant technical terminology
- Translate this terminology into the target language
- Have at hand (if by now you don't know it by heart) the equivalent — in the target language — of the legal English terminology: prior art, person skilled in the art, embodiment, etc., and the standard formulations of claims.

It looks easy. Now, the real difficulty is with terminology, as sometimes (always in the case of granted patents!) a patent describes a piece or a system that does not exist yet shows schematic drawings difficult to match with concrete words. This is why you have to understand the patent and have some background in its field. If things were simpler, machine translation would work quite well. But it doesn't, because machine translation does not keep consistency and it is not great at linking a term to its context as seen in the examples throughout this book.

The greatest difficulty with patent-related translations is that many agencies will just ask you to translate claims and will not have the whole original patent, so the above-mentioned rules cannot be applied. Taking such a job presents an ethical dilemma. If you take the job, it will take time to find the patents, apply the rules and figure out the right terminology for the claims. Nobody will pay for the time involved. If you don't take the job, somebody else will, for a lower price! The inexperienced are usually enthusiastic and there are many (most, in fact) agencies who will prefer what "sounds" good, over what is correct.

So, our advice is the following: accept patent and patent-related translations from agencies who are open to discussing the time involved in doing an accurate translation and ready to ask the client if there are questions. Be prepared to put a lot of time into it. It is a demanding, boring job (as no matter how exciting the idea, the core of a patent is repetition) and no matter how good a job you will do, nobody will appreciate it, which is understandable as it will read and sound like a patent, or worse, a patent claim — no, Proust would not be jealous!

### 4.13.1 *Exercises*

1. What is "a person skilled in the art"?
2. What are "claims"?
3. What is a "preferred embodiment"?

These are look-up questions and answers are not provided.

## 4.14 Contracts and Legal/Financial Translation

Neither of the authors of this book have any specific legal or accounting training and therefore this chapter is not intended to be a "How To" on this type of translation. Indeed, when offered such translations from agencies, if you do not have the prerequisite experience, it is best to politely say no. It is OK to say no to agencies, if you are:

- Not experienced in the field
- Too busy

The last thing they want is to receive a document that is:

- Inaccurate
- Does not use the correct terminology
- Mixes up terminology
- Sloppily done because you were rushed

As we have seen in the previous chapters on technical translation, each field has its own language and acronyms and if you are not using these correctly, your translation will seem amateurish if not downright unprofessional.

Having said that, often you cannot escape being faced with translations that are "legal" and/or "financial". This can happen if you are translating a contract that contains a lot of technical matter, for example the specifications for a nuclear power plant site, a building construction project, etc., as part of the document will have legal or financial implications.

These documents often cite various Laws (*Lois*), Decrees (*Décrets*), Orders (*Arrêtés*), and at least in France, these are accompanied by numbers and date when these acts were introduced into law. The key thing is accuracy so make sure you get these dates and numbers right. The same applies to financial parts where it is essential to be accurate with the numbers. CAT tools are especially useful here for they will tell you if you have your numbers wrong. This can be tedious especially if there are a lot of numbers but it is best not to ignore this point. Your client will not be forgiving.

Examples of terminology:

- *En application de* → "Pursuant to"
- *Actifs* → "Assets"
- *Passifs* → "Liabilities"

- *Participation* → "Share", "Stake", "Profit Sharing"
- *Actions* → "Shares" or "Stocks"
- *Obligations* → "Bonds"
- SAS (*Societé par Actions Simplifiée*) → "Joint Stock Company"
- *Echéance* → "Due date"

These are just a few typical terms that you will see repeatedly. Unfortunately, good bilingual dictionaries are scarce in these subjects so that is why you have to have a basic understanding of what is being referred to. (We have one rather thick French-to-English "Business" dictionary gathering dust on our shelves as it never has anything useful in it). Actually, when searching for terminology, it is often better to just go to a source language dictionary or a website that will explain what the term means and then figure out for yourself how you would translate it, with the help of the Internet where appropriate.

So bottom line is, if you have to, do your best but it will take a lot of effort if you don't happen to be trained in law or accounting. Otherwise, politely say no.

---

**Machine Translation Error 11**

An interesting "machine" translation in a call for tender document (*consultation*), where more than one company would be working in the same zone, translated:

*l'entreprise retardataire*

as

"the late company"

but meaning

"the delayed company"

with regard to how this would affect the other company. To call it the "late company" implies that it is "dead"!

### 4.14.1 *Exercises*

Find the correct translation for:

1. *Societé momentanée*
2. *TVA autoliquidation*
3. *Echéancier*
4. *Retribution*

# Chapter 5

# Translation As A Profession

## 5.1 General Issues Facing the Translator: Problems Encountered

The life of a translator is not always a happy one and you have to expect problems to arise. We shall assume that you are competent and have tried your best to produce a translation that is technically accurate and reflects well the subject matter in the source text. Let us assume that you have understood your subject and your terminology is correct and in context. Problems that can arise are the following:

1. The client thinks your translation is too literal. Too word-for-word. Why didn't you produce something different? Something... different.
2. We wanted something sexy, something 'Wow!' to draw the customer in.
3. That is not how we say it and we are the client so we know best.
4. You made a mistake in the title.
5. You made a spelling error on page 93.
6. You did not correct the Franglais in the source text (even though you were not paid to do so, and not even asked).
7. You told us you could do legal translations but you don't use standard legal terminology.
8. You used UK English but we wanted US English. Didn't we tell you? I am sure we did...

9. I don't think this was translated by a native English speaker.
10. I think the translator used machine translation.
11. The client pays the agency but the agency does not pay you.
12. You did the translation but the client does not exist.
13. The client overpays you and asks for you to return some of the money.

We shall deal with these problems individually. First, you must realise that clients are not always honest and problems 1–7 may be because they want to cut the price down and this is an excellent way to do it. The problem is you can never be sure if this is so or if you have simply not done the job they were looking for. Apparently, a past president of the United States is famous for not paying his service providers and makes the excuse that they did not do what he really wanted them to do. There is a local billionaire in our region who apparently does the same thing. Let's face it, you do not get rich being Mister or Mrs Nice Guy! OK we are griping here now but it is a question we have asked ourselves on a number of occasions.

### 5.1.1 *The client thinks your translation is too literal*

The problem here is that technical translations have to be accurate and this may mean that you should be literal. Of course, you do have to rephrase some sentences. For example, in French they often start a sentence with what an English person would end it with. But if you start rephrasing everything, you may be describing something totally different from what the author was saying. JBAM works with an agency that specialises in technical translations and they surveyed their clients to see what they want. 85% wanted accurate terminology. Style was secondary in many cases. But many other jobs require a level of literary skill. This is particularly true of websites and newsletters, common technical jobs. Personally speaking we have learned to stay well away from anything that involves "marketing" or "advertising". This is a specialty and is best done by translators who have a literary or business background. It is also very hard work and if you are not skilled in it, you will waste a lot of time trying to please the client who will inevitably not be pleased. Bottom-line, know what you are good at and what you are not good at. Believe me, the agency or client will be pleased if you say this as you will not be wasting their time either.

### 5.1.2 *We wanted something sexy...*

In other words, this is marketing. Selling something to someone who doesn't know they want it. You won't be able to win on this one if you are not trained in, what should we call it? Oh never mind...

### 5.1.3 *That is not how we say it*

This is an odd thing. We have worked with clients who have a particular vocabulary and they insist you use it. For example, we recently did a translation where there was a French acronym for a product used in biological controls of products. A type of culture medium. We had found the correct English equivalent for it from the multilingual website of the supplier, but the client insisted we stick with the French acronym. Another client insisted that in a maintenance manual, a fault was always referred to as a "failure" which makes things difficult when you want to say that something is "faulty".

In a situation like this, you should take the attitude: "the customer knows best". Don't try to fight it. It is them that are paying the bill and maybe they have used this terminology in lots of other documents and do not want it changed, to avoid confusion.

### 5.1.4 *You made a mistake in the title*

This is a really annoying thing to happen. Very often when doing a translation, you get so involved in getting the terminology right that you are careless about the "obvious". The problem is that titles are the most obvious thing in the outputted document and if you have made a mistake, it is what is called a "glaring error". Clients are very unforgiving about this for they think, if you were so careless with the title, maybe you were careless later on.

There is one thing here that you MUST look out for and that is text in capital (uppercase) letters. Generally, spellcheckers do not work with capital letters so it is very easy to make a silly mistake here. And it is often not even obvious. A word of advice here is that if you have to translate something that is in capitals in the source, write in in lowercase in the target and then change the case using your software (Word, Trados, MemoQ, etc.). If you have made a mistake, the spellchecker should find it.

### 5.1.5 *You made a spelling error on page 93*

This is very frustrating for on any size of document, it is easy to make a spelling error or bring in the wrong term from your termbase. The client is paying for the translation and they expect perfection. That is fair enough and you must do your best to avoid this happening. Use the spellchecker. Produce the output document so that you can read it through. We find that it is easy to miss things like this with CAT tools where the text is broken down into segments. And as we explained earlier in the book, if you have a spelling error that leads to a real word, the spellchecker will not find it. So, on the read-through, you must make sure your text makes sense.

It is also very difficult to find your own mistakes. A read-through by another person can be very useful though it is a time-consuming process for them.

### 5.1.6 *You did not correct the Franglais in the source text (even though you were not paid to do so, and not even asked)*

This is a real problem and in fact led us to lose our biggest customer. Sometimes you receive a document that is a mixture of untranslated text and text that has been translated by one of the employees who is "good at English". The problem is that often the "English" text is in very poor English with bad grammar and incorrect terminology. OK, you say, I can always clean this up and I am sure the original author will not mind. In the particular case we just mentioned, we were asked to translate a document where the agency said there were 30,000 words to do with a deadline four days ahead but in fact the document turned out to be 60,000 words. We ended up delivering the 30,000 words at 3 AM in the morning but did we get thanked? No. We didn't have time to correct the mess that the other 30,000 words were in but got blamed for them anyway. We have not worked with that agency since.

### 5.1.7 You told us you could do legal translations, but you don't use standard legal terminology

Who told you we could do legal translations but you sent the document anyway? Often when doing technical translations, in particular involving contracts, there will be segments that are legal in nature and these must be translated carefully to make sure you are saying exactly what is meant in the original document. Generally, we have found that this works out OK. We did have an example once though, when the document was the standard legal blurb attached to a document describing a piece of equipment. This is called boilerplate in the legal profession and often clients are charged for producing it even though it is standard and the same for everyone. Anyway, we did our best but it was not identical to what would normally be used and the final client was very difficult about it. Anyway, we did not get paid and will no longer work with that agency or that major corporation.

If in doubt, just say no.

### 5.1.8 You used UK English but we wanted US English. Didn't we tell you. I am sure we did...

If you are not sure, check with your agency or client. It happened once where we were informed halfway through a translation for a French company that they wanted the translation in US English.

Trying to go back and change all "s" to "z", etc., proved difficult and again the agency was unhappy. You should remember that the translator is at the bottom of the totem pole and generally will get the blame even though it may not have been your fault.

### 5.1.9 I don't think this was translated by a native English speaker

This is a comment that some clients like to throw out when they think your translation is too literal. It is very annoying if you happen to be a native English speaker. Really though, this notion of being a native XXX speaker is a bit of a nonsense. Many agencies have sought and obtained the famous ISO certification and one of the prerequisites for this is that they only work with native speakers. Just because you were born in a certain country does not mean that you necessarily have a good grasp of its language. Indeed, if you left the country early in life you may not speak that language at all. So what is your native language? Well, it is the language that you have learned to write in and master but legally this does not make you a native XXX speaker.

Of course, when you hand in a translation it should sound like what an English speaker would expect so in that sense it is a valid requirement. One of the points to consider though is to ask if the person making the comment is qualified to make it. Are they a native English speaker? In our experience, they are not. All comments of this type came from French native speakers! A word of warning: you will never fulfil the level of expectations of a French native speaker, even if the source documents is full of mistakes in their own language (no, we shall not give examples).

Here is maybe the place to complain about non-natives writing English source documents. One of us (AIFM) was often confronted with a really tricky issue: (very) poor source documents containing parts that were easily understood but others that were incomprehensible. All engineering, most of the time from German or Japanese companies. The first thing you notice when reading through is a lack of consistency in terminology. Then funny grammar and phrasing. Mixed with better parts (usually machine-translated parts). You tell the agency, who is always surprised, promises to tell the client, and encourages you to do your best. If you are lucky, at the client's end there is someone speaking good English, competent in their field, and willing to clarify and rephrase the really "killing" bits. If not, you highlight the problems, deliver a document with issues pointed out, and never hear again about what happened. You get paid, and thanked. Not so bad, from this point of view, but the actual translation is painful, time-consuming and leaves you frustrated.

### 5.1.10 *I think the translator used machine translation*

This is a statement that can accompany the previous problem or it may replace it. Again, clients have heard of Google Translate and they can use this as an excuse when they don't like your translation. To us as translators, this is the ultimate insult. We would never use machine translation as we are well aware of its limitations and frankly, proofreading machine translation is much more work that reading your own direct translation, so the concept is nonsense. Unless you don't mind handing in garbage.

We recently had a problem with a client who was a librarian in a university in eastern France and they didn't like the way we had translated a website. It was on a serious subject of direct relevance to professional researchers and concerned new ways of handling research data that had consequences from a funding point of view. The topic was rather dry and focused on instructions as to how to share open-source data.

Nevertheless they had the translation redone by someone who made it very snazzy and hip! We had produced a document that was factually correct and written in the language that a researcher would expect to see.

OK they were not happy and we didn't give them exactly what they imagined they wanted. But we were attacked in a series of angry e-mails directed to the head of the agency for whom we had done the work and who was the intermediate party. This librarian accused us of using machine translation and gave all sorts of examples where she fed in source sentences and came up with something very close to what

Google Translate produced. This was convincing for her. Then she threw out that she had shown the translation to an American friend and they thought it was not done by a native English speaker. "The works", as we say in English. In fact our work had been loaded onto a website so what was believed to be Machine Translation was actually our work that Google Translate had found!

Luckily this was an agency that we had worked with for ten years and the head of it realised that the complainer was "off her rocker", as we say in English. The fact is that we had been sent a Trados package for this translation. This is what agencies often use where the file to be translated is prepared so that it is directly injected into the CAT tool. As explained earlier in this book, this software is used to present the document broken down into segments in two columns, with the source in one column, and then you translate the "target" in the other column. We had used an older version of this that didn't include a machine translation feature so to have actually used machine translation, we would have had to copy out every segment into a text file, have it translated and then copy it back into the software. This would have taken much longer than straight translating. Hence, we could prove that we had not used machine translation since we did not have the original source file.

We, and the agency, were very angry about this, and the agency did not get paid the full agreed price for the job although we were paid. However, this librarian had potentially harmed our reputation and if we had not had a longstanding relationship with this agency, we could have suffered long-term financial harm. This was a very serious situation and we consulted a lawyer who confirmed what we believed, that we had been "slandered" (verbal defamation) and "libelled" (written defamation). The lawyer thought we had a good case and recommended suing the university. She even explained how we could finance this from our homeowner's insurance!

Maybe we could have gotten rich but in the end, we thought it was not worth it and let it drop. Still, it was something that breaks your heart when you try to do a good job and the client wants either to show their superiority, or maybe just does not want to pay for the work.

## 5.1.11 *The client pays the agency, but the agency does not pay you*

Back in early 2018, we were approached by an American agency, run by two French people, to do translations on the subject of insurance reports. This was fascinating work involving damage claims for property that had been destroyed or work that was substandard. We liked this job very much as it was not routine and we learned a lot about how dishonest people can be when making such claims. It was a real eye-opener to see major companies trying to pretend that their losses were much greater than could reasonably be claimed. The reports came in thick and fast, always with a very tight deadline, over a period of about three months. The first bill was paid on time, but when we put in a bill that amounted to about $7,000 we were surprised that the payment deadline passed without any sign of the money coming in. We had direct conversations with the lady who was the co-owner of the agency, and she said that there would be a delay, as they had some mix-up at the bank. As the months went by, we made many calls for payment and the response was very plaintive, telling us how things were so difficult and how the banks were totally unreasonable, etc. Eventually, after about a year, we contacted the original client who informed us that indeed they had paid this agency for the work. This was not their fault of course so we had no recourse with them.

Three years have gone by, but still no payment. The couple have moved back to France but the agency in the US is apparently still registered as a business. We since learned that we were not the only people to have worked for them and not been paid, even though they had previously a good reputation.

What most likely had happened was that husband had been taken ill and that as a result, their business's revenue had slumped, so they found the solution. They would get other people to do the translations and keep the money for themselves.

What recourse do we have? Frankly not much. The business is in the US so you would have to take them to court there which would be an expensive proposition.

Despite repeated assurances that we will eventually be paid, I think that we were really "stung" by this affair.

### 5.1.12 *You did the translation but the client does not exist*

This is a really odd thing that can happen, and it has happened to us on two occasions. The translation business works via the Internet and you get requests to do translations from people you really do not know. Generally the work comes from agencies and you can check their credibility on, for example, www.Proz.com.

One job came in when we were on a skiing holiday in the French Alps. This is very vivid in our memory as the file to be translated was very large and the Internet connection very bad because of the density of use in the ski resort. Eventually we had to download the file at 3 AM in the morning. The translation was done, sent to the contact person and the bill was sent to the agency. The reply came back… This person does not work for us. They had never heard of them. The translation was sent off into the aether and it is very hard getting the aether to pay. Apparently, we were not alone here either. Others had been cheated by this person who presumably had contracts to do translations and got others to do the work.

The second time, which was very recent, was for an agency and was a large translation about plant fertilizer. The work seemed to be a bit strange as there were dozens of products with little explanation why you should use one instead of another. There were some technical terms that were impossible to find. One was a "Ligerien" plant and the term "Ligerien" does exist but it means someone from the Loire Valley region in France. Some of the products were for growing marijuana plants. OK, why not… We did the job and sent in the bill. To our surprise a week or so later, the person from the agency contacted us to say that the client did not seem to exist. All communication with them had ceased and it was impossible to contact them. In this case we had both been cheated. Eventually we agreed to share the pain and we received half the agreed upon payment.

Again this is a hazard of working for people who appear from nowhere on the Internet and you do not have a way of establishing their true identity. Fortunately this kind of thing is rare and if you work with established agencies, you generally do not have this kind of trouble though in the second case, it was the agency who was cheated.

### 5.1.13 *The client overpays you and asks for you to return some of the money*

This was the most bizarre thing that happened to us. We were contacted by a client from Germany who had an Environmental Science document to be translated and we agreed on a price of €1,000. It was a big job. The client asked if it would be alright if he paid us by cheque. This was a first as we are normally paid by bank transfer or PayPal (if it is an American client). The job was done and the bill was sent. The person then explained that in fact he had been admitted to hospital and that a friend of his would make the payment. OK...

A registered letter arrives at our house and inside there were American Express traveller's checks for €3,000! Next we get an e-mail from the client to say that he is panicked as his friend had gotten the payments mixed up and had paid for his hospital bill instead of the translation bill, and could we send him back the difference to his address in South Africa. Now this was strange for we had thought that the person was in Germany.

We looked at the cheques and there was something that didn't quite seem right. We are very familiar with American Express traveller's cheques, but these ones didn't seem quite square. Let's have a look at the Internet. Eh *voila*... Scam.

You take the cheques to the bank and the young bank teller, without looking too close, deposits the money into your account. You are very touched by this hard-luck story of the poor man having had an operation and out of your natural human generosity, you send him the money so that he can pay his hospital bill.

A month later, American Express contacts your bank to say that these cheques are phony, and it will not honour them with the bank. The bank contacts you and tells you that the deposit they made on your behalf has been invalidated, so now you have just lost the €2,000 that you sent to Mr. X.

In fact, a lot of people have fallen for this and have been duly robbed.

Luckily, we have suspicious minds so off we went to the police station. It was the day before New Year's so we were told to come back in a couple of days when the financial expert would be there. Back on New Year's Day, the police officer says to us…Are you sure they are phony???

End of story. We didn't fall for the scam, but we had done one thousand euros' worth of translation for nothing. Time is money so we lost money and time!

There are many scams on the Internet and I am sure this is not the only one. So, the bottom line is, be careful who you work for you as you may end up being cheated and frankly, there is little way in which you can expect to gain compensation for such events. There is an expression in English: "Buyer Beware".

In this case it should be "Translator Beware".

## 5.2 Where to Find Work?

When we set out on this business, we prepared flyers and sent them to dozens of local businesses to see if they would take us on to do their translations for them. Sad to say, the result was zero.

But, all is not lost. There are companies on the Internet that act as clearing houses for translations and the one we work with is called ProZ. (Never sure if this is pronounced Pro-Z or Prose!). It is a company based in the United States and you can sign up with them as a member and put your profile on their site. They have a number of very useful features, one of which is their "Blue Book" which lists the agencies that use them along with a rating system as to the agency's reliability.

As we mentioned earlier in Section 3.5 on Internet Searching, they also have a kind of competition called Kudos where people ask for translations of terms and you can offer answers to these requests. In the early days of our membership, we participated a lot in this and won lots of "Kudos points". This was a way of getting known on the site.

# Final Words

The first part of this book is aimed at scientists and engineers writing articles destined for publication in journals, reports, etc., where the author writes directly in English (the lingua franca of this sector). The second part is aimed at professional translators undertaking this profession, whether starting out or seeking to expand their scope. We have not tried to present this as a grammar manual but rather to pass on to the reader what we have learned and our experience in both these activities. We hope that the reader will benefit from these words but especially that it will lead them to reflect on what they are doing. To understand where to find help when doing a translation in a field in which they are perhaps not totally familiar. To seek to understand what goes on in these different fields. What does the technology do? How is it handled? What are the issues involved? What are the most basic errors made when writing in English when it is not your native language? We also hope that you had some fun seeing the mistakes that can arise when machine translation is used out of context. And what to look out for.

There are many sectors we have not mentioned as these are areas that we do no work in: medicine, law, accounting, marketing and many more. You cannot do everything and probably you should not try if you are not comfortable in it.

We also did not discuss fields where we do a lot of work in, such as metallurgy, moulding, etc., as they are two-fold complicated:

a mixture of old, language-based vocabulary and advanced new technology which tends to be English-based. Maybe in a sequel to this book!

We would love to receive feedback on what we have presented here. What we have missed. What we could include in a future volume.

You can contact us directly at: merlrennes@merl-consulting.com.

# Additional Reading

1) Robert Burchfield, *Fowler's Modern English Usage*, Revised edition, Oxford University Press, 2004
2) Michael Swan, *Practical English Usage*, 4$^{th}$ edition, Oxford University Press, 2017
3) Robert Schoenfeld, *The Chemist's English*, 3$^{rd}$ edition, Wiley-VCH, 1989
4) Marc Défourneaux, *Do you speak science?: Comprendre et communiquer en anglaise scientifique*, Dunod, 2011

# Answers to Exercises

## Physics

1. *Moment cinétique* → momentum
2. *Coefficient directeur* → slope or gradient
3. *Tracé* → plot or graph plot
4. *Couple* → moment of force or torque
5. *Grandeur* → value or quantity

## Chemistry

1. *Gaz rare* is NOT "rare gas" (because Argon is not rare — 0.94% by volume of air) but "noble gas" (or, less accurately, "inert gas")
2. *Paillasse* is not "straw" but a "workbench"
3. REACH stands for Registration, Evaluation & Authorisation of Chemicals
4. *Témoin* → control standard
5. *Solution-mère* → parent solution
6. *Squelette carboné* → carbon skeleton
7. *Taux de réaction* → reaction rate

## Aeronautics

1. *Empennage* → horizontal stabiliser or empennage
2. *Turbopropulseur* → turboprop engine

3. *Train avant (TAV)* → nose gear
4. *Sauterelle* → cowling fastener

## Automotive Engineering

1. *Fusée de l'essieu* → axle journal bearing
2. *Volant moteur* → flywheel
3. *Durite* → hose

## Railways and Trams

1. *Canton* → block, signalling block, or section (designated section of track; see: https://maligne-ter.com/tours-orleans-paris/2019/11/05/les-fondamentaux-de-la-sncf-le-canton-le-circuit-de-voie-et-la-signalisation/)
2. *Carré* → signal
3. *Clé Berne* → Berne key (key carried by train agent used to open panels, doors, etc.; can be square or triangular)

## Mechanical Engineering

1. *Magnétoscopie (MT)* → Magnetic Particle Inspection (MPI)
2. *Mep UT* → Ultrasonic Thickness Testing
3. *Traitement thermique après soudage (TTAS)* → Post-Welding Heat Treatment (PWHT)
4. *CND* → NDT (non-destructive testing)
5. *Rondelle griffe* → shakeproof washer
6. *Pas de pèlerin soudage* → backstep welding
7. *Chaude de retrait* → flame straightening
8. *Pièce martyre* → sacrificial part
9. *TOFD UT PA* → time-of-flight diffraction ultrasonic thickness testing

## Construction

1. *Tel que construit (TQC)* → as-built
2. *Bon pour execution (BPE)* → approval to proceed

3. *Escalier helicoidal* → spiral staircase
4. *Nomenclature* → bill of materials
5. *Economiste de la construction* → quantity surveyor

**Nuclear Engineering**

1. *Tranche* → nuclear plant unit
2. *Anthropogammétrie* → whole-body gamma measurement (or counting)
3. *Réfrigérant atmosphérique* → cooling tower
4. *Essai hydraulique* → hydrostatic test or hydrotest

**Renewable Energy**

1. *Poste de transformation électrique* → electricity sub-station
2. *Evacuation d'énergie* → power transmission

**Hydroelectric Power and Hydraulic Engineering**

1. *Electrovanne* → solenoid valve
2. *Caloporteur* → cooling fluid
3. *Structures émergées et structures immergées* → above surface and submerged structures
4. *Vanne guillotine* → gate valve

**Contracts and Legal/Financial Translation**

1. *Societé momentanée* → joint venture
2. *TVA autoliquidation* → VAT reverse charge
3. *Echéancier* → payment schedule
4. *Retribution* → renumeration

# Appendix I

## Original Text of the Claude-Levy Strauss Quotation

*Pour former ce recueil, je me suis heurté à une difficulté sur laquelle je dois appeler l'attention du lecteur. Plusieurs de mes articles ont été écrits directement en anglais, il fallait donc les traduire. Or, au cours du travail, j'ai été frappé par la différence de ton et de composition entre les textes conçus dans l'une ou l'autre langue. Il en résulte une hétérogénéité qui, je le crains, compromet l'équilibre et l'unité de l'ouvrage.*

*Cette différence s'explique sans doute, en partie, par des causes sociologiques : on ne pense et on n'expose pas de la même façon, quand on s'adresse à un public français ou anglo-saxon. Mais il y a aussi des raisons personnelles. Quelle que soit mon habitude de la langue anglaise, dans laquelle j'ai enseigné plusieurs années, je l'utilise de façon incorrecte et dans un registre limité. Je pense en anglais ce que j'écris dans cette langue, mais, sans m'en rendre toujours compte, je dis ce que je peux avec les moyens linguistiques dont je dispose, non ce que je veux. D'où le sentiment d'étrangeté que j'éprouve en présence de mes propres textes, quand j'essaye de les retranscrire en français.*

— Claude Levy-Strauss, Anthroplogie structurale,
Préface, Pocket, Plon, 2016

# Appendix II

AIFM regularly post-edits a machine-translated chemistry course from English into French and this is a rich source of translation errors but also serves to illustrate many basic translation issues. We have left this to the appendix so as not to create confusion from the French-to-English translation used for examples and discussion in the body of the text.

| | |
|---|---|
| Like many metals, iron is ductile and can be drawn into a wire, which discounts answer A. | Comme beaucoup de métaux, le fer est ductile et peut être attiré par un fil, ce qui réduit la réponse à A [correct : ce qui élimine la réponse A]. |
| One of the simplest reactions involves red-hot iron reacting with either dry air or oxygen to produce magnetic iron(II, III) oxide: <chem> | L'une des réactions les plus simples consiste à faire réagir du fer brûlant [correct : fer chauffé à blanc] avec de l'air sec ou de l'oxygène pour produire de l'oxyde de fer magnétique (II, III) : <chem> |

| | |
|---|---|
| Humans have been continuously alloying different pure metal elements for what seems to be all of recorded history because alloying is a relatively simple process that can transform a relatively non-useful metal into a much more useful metallic composite substance. | L'homme a sans cesse allié différents éléments de métal pur à travers toute l'histoire recensée, car l'alliage est un procédé relativement simple qui peut transformer un métal relativement inutile en une substance composite métallique beaucoup plus utile [correct : en un bien plus utile composé métallique]. |

Composite material = matériau composé not matériau composite !

| | |
|---|---|
| It is important to understand the difference between accuracy and precision. | Il est important de comprendre la différence entre la précision [correct : exactitude] et la précision.<br><br>*Put like that, it would be certainly a difficult difference to grasp!* |
| It is possible to be both precise and inaccurate and it is possible to be both accurate and imprecise. | Il est possible d'être à la fois précis et imprécis [correct : inexact], et il est possible d'être à la fois précis [correct : exact] et imprécis.<br><br>*This one is a gem, don't hold your breath, you don't always get so much fun!* |
| The following illustration shows a triangle with attractive forces existing between oppositely charged ions and repulsion between ions with like charges. | L'illustration suivante montre un triangle avec des forces d'attraction existant entre des ions chargés de manière opposée [correct : ayant des charges opposées] et une répulsion entre des ions ayant des charges semblables [correct : du même signe]. |

|  | *Like*: Not *"similar"* which would be meaningless here, nor *"identical"* because only the sign matters; *like* means *"of the same kind"*, and that means here either positive or negative. |
|---|---|
| Iron makes up 5.63% of Earth's crust | Le fer se maquille [correct : constitue] 5.63 de la croûte terrestre, |
| The first period 4d-block element we will examine is scandium | La première période que nous examinerons est un élément de bloc 4d [Correct : le premier élément du bloc d de la période 4 que nous allons étudier] est le scandium, *Here is where the algorithm starts to have a mind of its own…* |

Fighter jets ≠ chasseurs de combat [correct: avions de chasse]
Water gas ≠ gaz de l'eau [correct: gaz à l'eau]

| To allow the buret to be filled while sitting down | Laisser la burette s'asseoir [correct: Afin de vous permettre de remplir la burette en restant assis] |
|---|---|
| The hydroxide ions interact with the halogenoalkane molecules and new alcohol products are produced as the carbon–halogen bond breaks through fission processes. | Les ions hydroxyde interagissent avec les molécules d'halogénoalcanes et de nouveaux produits alcooliques sont obtenus lorsque la liaison carbone-halogène traverse [correct : se rompt à cause de] les processus de dissociation. *This is where the source is wrong!!!* |

| When transferring substances from one vessel to another, we can use a stem funnel, shown below, to prevent spills. | Lors du transfert de substances d'un navire [correct : récipient] à un autre, nous pouvons utiliser un entonnoir à tige, illustré ci-dessous, pour éviter les déversements. *Easy to oversee, as it makes sense if you do not think!!!* |
|---|---|
| These plants are usually located near coasts, roads, and railway lines. | Ces plantes [correct : usines] sont généralement situées à proximité des côtes, des routes et des lignes de chemin de fer. *This makes perfect sense; you could easily miss it!* |
| A student dissolves \<quantity\>\<value\>25\</value\>\<unit\>gram\</unit\>\</quantity\> of \<chem\> into water to produce a solution with a volume of \<quantity\>\<value\>500\</value\>\<unit\>centimeter^3\</unit\>\</quantity\>. | Un étudiant se dissout [correct : dissout] \<quantity \>\<value\> 25\</value\>\<unit\> gram\</unit\>\</quantity\> de\<chem\> dans l'eau pour produire une solution avec un volume de\<quantity \>\<value\> 500\</value\>\<unit\>centimeter^3 \</unit\>\</quantity\>. *Needless to say that albeit awful, this would be an unusual experience!* |

(electronic) shell: coque, coquille, obus, enveloppe, shell, case, réservoir — all in one text!!! And of course, no couche, not even once!

| Neither of these species are charged. | Aucune de ces espèces n'est accusée [correct : chargée]. |
|---|---|

Printed by Amazon Italia Logistica S.r.l.
Torrazza Piemonte (TO), Italy

52723351R00107